1213895213

# WORLD GRAPHIC DESIGN

# WORLD
# GRA

# PHIC DESIGN

CONTEMPORARY GRAPHICS FROM AFRICA, THE FAR EAST, LATIN AMERICA AND THE MIDDLE EAST

## GEOFFREY CABAN

**MERRELL**

First published 2004 by Merrell Publishers Limited

Head office
42 Southwark Street
London SE1 1UN

New York office
49 West 24th Street
New York, NY 10010

www.merrellpublishers.com

**Publisher** Hugh Merrell
**Editorial Director** Julian Honer
**US Director** Joan Brookbank
**Sales and Marketing Director** Emilie Amos
**Sales and Marketing Executive** Emily Sanders
**Design Manager** Nicola Bailey
**Managing Editor** Anthea Snow
**Editor** Sam Wythe
**Production Manager** Michelle Draycott

British Library Cataloguing-in-Publication Data:
Caban, Geoffrey
World graphic design : contemporary graphics from Africa, the Far East,
Latin America and the Middle East
1.Graphic arts – Africa 2.Graphic arts – East Asia 3.Graphic arts –
Latin America 4.Graphic arts – Middle East
I.Title
741.6

ISBN 1 85894 219 5

Produced by Merrell Publishers Limited
Commissioned by Mark Fletcher
Designed by Hoop Design
Edited by Kate Blake with Laura Hicks
Indexed by Laura Hicks
Printed and bound in Hong Kong

**PAGE 7**
Contents page for an issue of the rock magazine *La Mosca*:
Edgar Reyes Ramírez, Mexico, 2002
**PAGE 17 (and jacket, top)**
Cover for the annual report of a conservation organization:
Chaz Maviyane-Davies, Zimbabwe, 1998
**PAGE 18**
Calendar for a fruit and fruit-juice processing and packaging
company in Nairobi: Ajmeet Bharij, Kenya, 2002
**PAGE 41 (and jacket, second from top)**
Serigraphic (silkscreen) print: Kum Nam Baik, Korea, 2001
**PAGE 42**
Poster from a series of nine entitled 'We Are One':
Fang Chen, China, 1997–2000
**PAGE 85 (and jacket, second from bottom)**
Postcard from the series 'Usted no está aquí' (You are not here):
Edgar Reyes Ramírez, Mexico, 2001
**PAGE 86**
Poster for the Latin American Association of Design:
Pablo Kunst, Argentina, 1998
**PAGE 129 (and jacket, bottom)**
Typography for a typography-exhibition poster:
Majid Abbasi, Iran, 2003
**PAGE 130**
*Afraid of God*, a poster on a religious/political theme:
Extrastruggle (Memed Erdener), Turkey, 2001

# 6 INTRODUCTION

# 6 INTRODUCTION

2

1

THE INTENTION OF THIS BOOK IS TO explore the richness and variety of graphic imagery that has developed outside the influence of the 'European tradition', focusing on the work of graphic designers and artists in four geographical zones: Africa, the Far East, Latin America and the Middle East. The visual traditions in these regions have been shaped by many factors, including religion, mythology and politics, as well as by the tools and materials locally available, and these influences have resulted in some particularly distinctive approaches to visual communication. These are reflected in posters, magazines, comics, record covers, packaging and various forms of promotion, and are also apparent in a range of vernacular graphic expression that includes graffiti, street murals, transport decoration, signs, political symbols, and textiles and fashion imagery.

When applied to graphic design, the term 'European tradition' implies that the design has a standardized, international form. The origins of this tradition can be traced back to the establishment by Walter Gropius of the Bauhaus in Germany in the 1920s, and the subsequent spread of Bauhaus design principles to the USA and most parts of the developed world. Among the influences contributing to the development of this 'European tradition' have been the 'Swiss style' of typography, developed by Joseph Muller-Brockman and Max Bill in the late 1950s, and the establishment of international creative

departments by the large multinational advertising agencies. In addition, the international popularity of such magazines as *Graphis, Gebrauchsgraphik, Domus, Fortune, Esquire* and *Print* has been responsible for the worldwide adoption of certain approaches to layout, illustration and typography. In recent years, the most far-reaching changes have been brought about by the introduction of digital imaging and software programs such as Photoshop and Illustrator. Although these have introduced graphic designers to new ways of thinking, and have generally been welcomed, they have also contributed to a decline in the use of 'wet' photography and hand-drawn and illustrated work.

It is difficult to find examples of visual communication that have not been touched in some way by new technologies and international design approaches. Many of the designers whose work is represented in this book felt it necessary, for various reasons, to undertake their design education abroad. Some completed their studies at leading design schools in the USA, Europe and the UK before returning to practise in their own countries. Having honed their skills and acquired a grasp of international approaches and technologies, they were often disappointed to find on their return that many of the visual traditions of their homeland were being lost.

One of the objectives of this book is to portray the views of the contributing designers on two key topics: the major influences that have been instrumental to

4

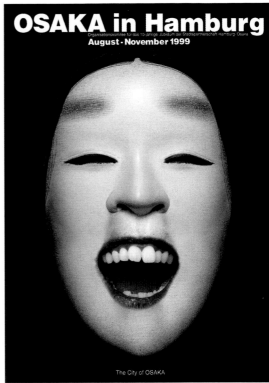

5

their development and approach as graphic designers; and the aspects of graphic design in their own countries that they feel are particularly distinctive. Most believe that the indigenous art and iconography of their homeland has had a significant influence on their work. Designers from Iran speak of the thousands of years of visual traditions that have shaped contemporary approaches to design in their country, and give as examples the calligraphy and textile patterns of pre-Islamic civilizations, as well as miniature painting, ceramic tiles and Persian carpets. In China, Fang Chen's design for a pack of modern playing cards was inspired by the Figure Cards of Heroes of the Water Margin Chronicles by the seventeenth-century Chinese painter Lao-lian Chen. Taiwanese designer Su Tsung-Hsiung has drawn upon the cursive style of Hsing Tsao, a Taiwanese calligrapher from the Ching dynasty, while the posters of U.G. Sato of Japan have been influenced greatly by the Ukiyo-e woodcut printing of the Edo

period. Indigenous influences on designers from Latin America have come from pre-Hispanic native ornament and handicrafts, African art, and more recent iconology such as the gauchos and the mate of Argentina. According to Zimbabwean designer Saki Mafundikwa, Picasso's inspiration for Cubism sprang from the traditional masks of Africa, and this was the beginning of modern graphic design.

Although the history of modern graphic design in most of the regions covered in this book is relatively short, some pioneering figures have been named as having a considerable influence on contemporary approaches. Among these are the Iranians Morteza Momayez and Farshid Mesghali, the Brazilian Aloisio Magalhaes, the Cuban poster designer Raúl Martínez, the Mexican Germán Montalvo, Indian designer Aurobind Patel and Yusaka Kamekura of Japan.

Inspiration has been drawn also from non-visual arenas. Politics, religion, social justice and sustainability have provided strong motivation for

3

6

Questions relating to the second objective of this book, which is to focus on distinctive elements of design from each region, drew mixed responses from designers. Graphic designers, like many creative people, are fond of discussing whether the work produced in their country or locality has a distinguishable style and quality. Many of them argued that it is futile to talk about national design styles, and stressed that design is now 'global'. Colombian designer Professor David Consuegra believes that, although there is no such thing as a distinctive Colombian style of graphic design, it is possible to identify a number of native design elements that are characteristic of the graphic expression of Latin America. This observation can be applied to all the regions represented in the book, and some general comments can be made about the forms of native visual expression of each one.

Some characteristics of Middle Eastern design are easily identifiable: brilliant colours, intricate geometric patterns and beautiful calligraphy. The images produced by graphic designers of Arab origin often have special levels of meaning, driven by religious and cultural impulses.

Graphic design in countries that lie south of the Sahara Desert in Africa has been strongly influenced by mythology, oral traditions and the materials of the local environment. For centuries Sub-Saharan designers and artists have drawn inspiration from the

many designers in this book, and their views on particular issues are expressed in powerful visual forms. Some have taken their ideas from philosophy, literature and music. Nearly all are very familiar with international design trends and approaches as a result of both their educational and professional experience and their exposure to international magazines, conferences and global media. Many contemporary international graphic designers and artists have been named as important influences.

*Las olas, las olas*
*que vienen y vienen y luego se van,*
*se cruzan, se cruzan y luego se juntan,*
*y se vuelven grandes y se vuelven chicas,*
*y se vuelven verdes, azules y blancas.*
*Al verse un barquito que lejos ya va,*
*parece que fueran las olas el cielo*
*y lento, muy lento, cruzara un lucero.*

7

images of spirits. Traditional stories, passed by word of mouth from generation to generation, credit the ancestor spirit with initiating many forms of design and craft. Consequently, spiritual themes are represented in much of the vernacular visual imagery from this region.

Latin American graphic design is often characterized by the use of indigenous ornamental motifs that are carved, painted or cut out, and that have similar compositional elements. Design from different zones within a country can sometimes be identified by the distinctive use of certain patterns, particularly zigzags, squares and circles.

When discussing graphic design in the Far East, we tend to focus on developments in Japan and China, although a rich visual heritage is evident in India, Taiwan and other countries. The growth of graphic design in Japan in the past fifty years has mirrored the country's accelerated economic development during this period, while in China political leaders have often determined the roles of designers and artists. In contrast to the emphasis

on *katachi* (form) in Japanese design, graphic design in China has been generally characterized by *qi* (formlessness).

One measure of the skill of graphic designers from the 'non-European tradition' is the success with which they combine indigenous iconography with contemporary approaches and techniques. Some advocate caution, expressing their dislike for the inappropriate or kitsch use of indigenous imagery. Indian designer Itu Chaudhuri feels that Indian designers will become increasingly international in their approaches as the country globalizes. While respecting the incorporation of traditional Indian imagery in appropriate circumstances, he is wary of the presentation of Indian visual clichés in ways that are "condescending or annoyingly Orientalist". Some justification for Chaudhuri's view is provided by Ticio Escober in a paper published in *Beyond the Fantastic: Contemporary Art Criticism from Latin America* (1995, p. 91). Escober writes: "One of the most characteristic myths of the Western world is that popular art, especially if it is indigenous, should remain the same, stuck in the past. Petrified in its most picturesque manifestations, popular art becomes a surviving relic of an archaic world, a miraculous link with nostalgic pasts and distant places." South African designer Garth Walker believes that African design should reflect African rather than Eurocentric origins. Through his studio

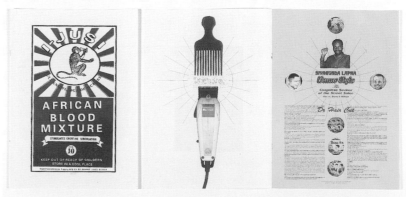

9

magazine, *i-jusi*, Walker has embarked on the development of "a new design language rooted in the African tradition" that draws upon "the visual imagery of the stuff around us – typography, colours, calligraphy and illustration".

The advantages offered to graphic designers by digital technology and software packages are almost impossible to ignore. A few of the participating designers consider Photoshop and Illustrator simply to be agents for the erosion of traditional craft skills in illustration, typography and photography. Most, however, appear to appreciate that the digital world offers new approaches to design, and innovative ways of combining traditional imagery with contemporary themes. Su Tsung-Hsiung of Taiwan has successfully mixed traditional and contemporary themes and techniques in his poster series 'The dialog between dancers and calligraphy'. His

visual tools are the Chinese writing brush and the computer, and his theme is informed by traditional Chinese folk religion, architecture and music.

Among the challenges facing graphic designers in some countries is the task of communicating visually to populations of mixed cultures who speak different languages. As Singapore designer Jackson Tan notes, his country is traditionally a Malay island with a Chinese ancestry that was colonized by the British. Halim Choueiry points out that in his country, Lebanon, there are three major languages, Arabic, French and English, and that these can sometimes co-exist in a work of design. Vietnamese and Laotian designers need to communicate in French as well as their native tongue. As Choueiry notes, these situations provide opportunities for distinctive approaches to graphic design.

It became apparent during the course of research

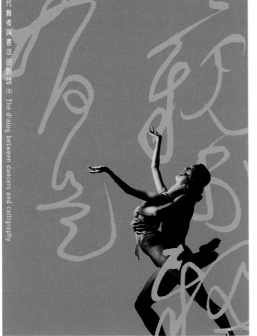

13

for this book that most of the participating designers feel strongly that they have the potential to influence social change. Indeed, many believe that the struggle for social change is an integral part of their mission as designers. Memed Erdener of Turkey insists that his name appears as 'Extrastruggle' on his work. Through this signature Erdener is stating his commitment not only to political reform in Turkey but also to the adoption of new thought processes that can bring this about. "I dream of the real Istanbul being very different from, and at the same time identical to, the road signs that welcome strangers to the city," he says. The work of Brazilian designer Veronica d'Orey reflects her commitment to design for sustainability, and she endeavours to use themes and approaches that focus on the threatened Brazilian rainforests. Occasionally this brings her into conflict with clients who are looking for a more "hi-tech feel".

Zimbabwean designer Chaz Maviyane-Davies has used the international awareness he acquired through years of study and practice in England in the 1970s to address humanitarian and political problems in Zimbabwe. "While at college in England I was always aware of my background and the role I hoped to play when I returned to an independent Zimbabwe," he says. "I was influenced by the graphics of nations in situations similar to mine, especially Cuban posters. Through their colour, courage and vibrancy they expressed a freedom and vigour I knew existed somewhere in my subconscious. They spoke of liberation, dignity and identity. My knowledge of this, acquired during my time abroad, helped me to develop my personal style of expression."

The zealous pursuit of political, social and environmental causes by graphic designers is not confined, of course, to those from non-European regions. Victor Margolin looks at the power of the graphic designer as a social revolutionary in his book *The Struggle for Utopia: Rodchenko, Lissitzky, Moholy-Nagy, 1917–1946* (1997), which focuses on the work of the European artists/designers Alexander Rodchenko, El Lissitzky and Laszlo Moholy-Nagy. According to Margolin, they wanted nothing less than to bring about utopia through the practice of art and design. Despite the failure of their ambitions in Hitler's Germany, Stalin's Russia and Eastern Europe, "the artistic-social avant-garde's extraordinary determination to infuse psychic and social power into their art, often in spite of external forces that sought

14

to minimize it, remains exemplary" (p. 251).

In an address to the National Design Conference of the American Institute of Graphic Arts (AIGA) in March 2002, Steven Heller spoke on "graphic intervention, or how designers critically redress the social, political and cultural grievances of the day". He argued that in the aftermath of 11 September 2001, political satire in American cartoons and other forms of expression was replaced by "unambiguous heroic realism" of a kind not seen since the Second World War. "While we mourned the dead and celebrated the heroes," said Heller, "some of us – perhaps many of us – had a disturbing sense that not just irony but also dissent was falling victim to fear." Heller maintained that the role of graphic intervention is to hold leaders accountable for their actions.

It can be argued that designers from non-European regions engage more constantly in social and political causes than do those from the West. Although there are many exceptions, 'European' designers tend to become involved in such campaigns on a periodic basis (for instance, the 2003 war in Iraq resulted in a flood of anti-war poster design from all corners of the Earth) only to return again to designing corporate brochures for multinational companies. This may be because the struggle against social injustice in some non-European countries is ongoing, or there is less pressure to balance "graphic intervention" and "unambiguous heroic realism",

as Heller has called it, or it may be because less emphasis is currently placed upon material concerns and pursuits in these countries.

It will not be possible in this book to recognize the work of all the graphic designers who have contributed to the development of the visual tradition in their countries. The fact that there are relatively few women designers represented here does not reflect any editorial views on comparative work quality or standards. It reflects, rather, the very small number of women graphic designers who became available for participation after searches through professional design associations and by word of mouth. Perhaps this demonstrates one similarity between graphic designers of 'European' and 'non-European' traditions: despite women being in the majority in graphic-design courses internationally, and the large numbers of talented women entering design practice, it is still difficult for them to develop high profiles.

It is not the intention of this book to profile only the 'best' work from the various regions, although many of the designers represented have strong international reputations. By selecting designers and examples of work that reflect interesting and significant developmental stages, I have endeavoured to offer an appreciation of the approaches these designers have adopted, and of the factors that have influenced them.

No más presos
sin sentencia

14 Invitation to an exhibition of household
items: Ajmeet Bharij, Kenya, 2001
15 Poster opposing 'imprisonment without
sentencing' for the Corporation of Latin-
American Development: Antonio Mena,
Ecuador, 1994
16 Greetings card: Reza Abedini, Iran,
2003
17 Logo for Brazilian jewellery created
from seeds from the Amazonian
rainforest: Veronica d'Orey, Brazil,
2002

16

17

1

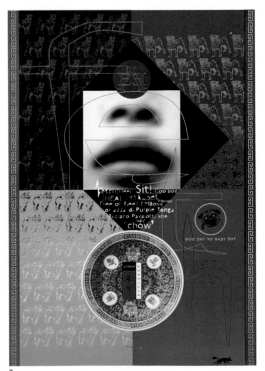

2

ALTHOUGH THE COUNTRIES LYING SOUTH of the Sahara Desert have long and proud visual traditions, particularly in relation to vernacular craftwork and imagery based on spiritual themes, the profession of graphic design in these countries is relatively new. Only a few of the larger cities in southern Africa, including Johannesburg, Capetown and Durban in South Africa and Harare in Zimbabwe, have the levels of manufacturing industry and international trade that provide significant opportunities for graphic designers. The creative departments of a few advertising agencies operating in these cities undertake much of the graphic design for the larger companies and their products, and the need for the products to have global appeal is often reflected in the 'Western' approach of the design of promotional material and packaging.

Graphic designers in Africa who work outside the advertising agencies may undertake some corporate work, but tend to focus upon projects of a cultural or humanitarian nature. The studio of Zimbabwean designer Chaz Maviyane-Davies is fairly typical of the smaller design studios in African cities. Maviyane-Davies once employed eight people but now prefers to work alone with a few select clients that are mainly non-government agencies. His work includes corporate identities and annual reports, as well as book and magazine design, and he is known internationally for his posters on human rights issues.

"Most of my work is local, though some of the more interesting commissions come from abroad," says Maviyane-Davies. "While there is a shortage in Zimbabwe of skilled resources to draw from in my daily work, I have a close relationship with a couple of photographers and other artists with whom I can work closely to achieve my objectives."

A career as a graphic designer in Sub-Saharan Africa is more difficult for those who work outside the large centres of southern Africa. Nigerian graphic designer 'Segun Olude explains how economic conditions affect his profession: "Our resources have been depleted in recent years and people use what they can find," he says. On the other hand, Ajmeet Bharij, a designer for an advertising agency in Nairobi, Kenya, finds that her clients range from those who want low-budget work to corporate clients "who will pay top-dollar". Graphic designers in the Sub-Saharan region remain acutely aware that, while vernacular imagery will be produced in any socio-economic environment, graphic design tends to flourish only where the industrial infrastructure is strong.

Some of the freelance graphic-design studios in Sub-Saharan Africa are endeavouring to reflect African themes and approaches in their work. Garth Walker of Orange Juice Design in Durban, South Africa, estimates that 99% of all graphic design and advertising in Southern Africa is currently

'Eurocentric' in approach, and he urges designers to develop a new design language that draws upon the "stuff around us – the vernacular typography, colours, calligraphy, and illustration". Walker points to certain visual traditions that are rooted in African history, and includes the fondness of black Africans for gothic lettering and 'special effects' in their visual language, which is reflected in the excesses of their clothing, houses and vehicles. These traditions have influenced Walker's own work, as can be seen from the illustrations and typography in his studio magazine *i-jusi*.

There is an abundance of traditional iconography in the lands below the Sahara, where art objects have always been an integral part of life. Historically, much African art has been linked to spiritual beliefs, and elaborately designed masks and painted figures have been used to connect to ancestral and nature spirits. There is a further connection between the nature spirits and Africa's unique landscapes, and graphic designers are clearly aware of their good fortune in being able to draw on this inheritance as a visual resource.

When African graphic designers are asked to name visual elements that characterize their region, they all agree on at least one of them. "Colours, colours, colours," says Zimbabwean designer Saki Mafundikwa, who goes on to explain that the colours of Africa reflect its heat, natural environment, human qualities

and conflicts. Nigerian designer 'Segun Olude says that he is constantly struggling with the use of colour in his professional life, sometimes embracing the vibrant colours of Africa and sometimes avoiding them. According to Kenyan designer Ajmeet Bharij, the colours of Kenya have always informed the country's arts and crafts traditions. Garth Walker of South Africa nominates colour, along with typography and illustration, as the basis for his vision of "a new design language rooted in the African tradition".

Walker's view of the importance of vernacular visual imagery to graphic design in Africa is supported by other designers. Michael Stallenberg of the studio Interactive Africa in Capetown says that his visual education has been shaped by "the people who do the signs for their barbershop, or those who imitate the Coca-Cola or Nike logos on the back of their cars". Saki Mafundikwa believes that African vernacular imagery has provided inspiration not just for people of the African continent but also for designers and artists of all countries. "It's all here," he asserts. "This is the source of it all. Africa is the birthplace of all humanity." Ajmeet Bharij, faced with the challenge of reflecting the national culture of Kenya in a calendar for a tinned-fruit manufacturer, reproduced the fruit tins in the forms of vernacular jewellery. 'Segun Olude points out that one feature of indigenous culture in Africa with implications for

4

designers is the appeal of the direct visual image. "Nothing is masked or given a double meaning," he explains. "Everything is immediate, especially when it comes to informational posters and public messages. For example, the most effective way for a designer to illustrate a murder would be to show a knife stuck in someone's chest."

African graphic designers generally agree that pressures to adopt Western lifestyles and attitudes have contributed to a decline in the use of vernacular imagery in contemporary graphic design. Johannesburg-based designer Roy Clucas is one who is not particularly unhappy about this. "On the local scene, we are all dabbling with reducing and flavouring this emerging cross-cultural soup that might one day become a distinctively South African style," he says. "The truth is I'm not a huge fan of nationalistic or societal territorialism. Exploring visual expression is a broader pursuit than that in my book, as unpopular as that may sound to many folk across the planet."

Other designers lament the loss of cultural icons in the African visual language. Chaz Maviyane-Davies believes that the icons and visual manifestations of Zimbabwean traditions are increasingly considered to be inferior as Africans readily adopt global lifestyles and attitudes. He explains: "I basically believe that in our quest for 'progress' we have relegated huge chunks of their indigenous culture into recesses of our subconscious instead of using it to define our role in the world we want to live in. We must adapt and develop our traditions and values to suit us, using a symbolism and visual language that is not only meaningful to us but also enriching to a world that has run out of ideas other than market forces (the new world order)."

Since the 1960s the theme of political struggle has been prominent in art and design that has focused on Africa. The national and international campaigns against apartheid in South Africa gained momentum from this time and led to the Soweto riots in 1976, the 'rent and service' boycotts of the 1980s, the State of Emergency declared by the government, and ultimately to the democratic election of a representative government in 1994. The post-colonial histories of other Sub-Saharan countries, including Zimbabwe, have been marked by struggles over independence, human rights issues, and land and property rights. As a result of the limited opportunities for freedom of expression within some

**The Man His Words His Life**

MITCHELL KRUGEL

JORDAN

5

of these countries, the social and political battles have often been taken up by designers and artists living outside the countries.

Philip Meggs in *A History of Graphic Design* (1992) wrote that, as a result of international solidarity posters opposing apartheid in South Africa from the late 1960s, "by default, a South African graphic heritage is being formed by artists outside the nation's boundaries". Meggs explained that the posters were not created in South Africa during this period because it was illegal to produce anti-government graphics, and the black majority lacked access to art training and printing materials. The struggle against apartheid was taken up by graphic artists in countries including Cuba and the United States, and within Europe.

In her introduction to *Resistance Art in South Africa* (1989), Sue Williamson contends that this situation began to change in the late 1970s when "there was a growing realization among anti-apartheid forces (within South Africa) that cultural resistance was a tool of immense power". As a result, according to Williamson, an increasing number of South African designers began to produce posters and graphics that expanded public consciousness of the issue. Campaigns based on human rights, health and political topics continue in some African countries, and while a number of graphic designers are still forced to maintain their involvement in campaigns

from abroad, others have found ways to contribute from within their own countries. The strong social conscience of designers from the region is apparent in both corporate and cultural projects, and this social conscience is projected in varied and often subtle ways. To take just one example, the humorous and seemingly light-hearted work of Durban designer Garth Walker is laced with irony and powerful social messages.

The graphic-design profession tends to flourish in countries where tertiary design education is freely available and design practitioners are supported by active professional organizations. While tertiary design education is now available in many countries in Sub-Saharan Africa, support from professional bodies is not. Design South Africa (DSA) and the Regroupement des Graphistes et Sérigraphes de Kinshasa (RGSK) from the Republic of the Congo are the only professional graphic-design associations from Sub-Saharan Africa that are listed as affiliates of the International Council of Graphic Design Associations (Icograda). Graphic designers from southern Africa are able to benefit from the professional activities and conferences facilitated by the DSA, and the profession in other African countries would benefit from the establishment of similar associations.

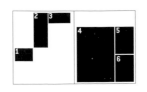

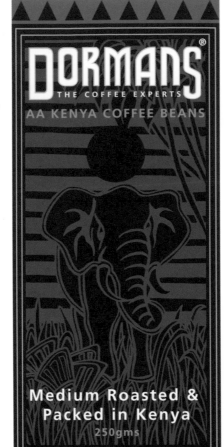

**AJMEET BHARIJ**

AJMEET BHARIJ IS A GRAPHIC designer at the TBWA/CREATIVE studio in Nairobi, Kenya. Her design education began in the late 1990s with a short course in computer applications in design at a college in Nairobi, after which she worked for a printer, where she learned much about print technology and the printing process. During an apprenticeship at Anvil Design Works she began practising graphic design while also receiving valuable tuition from her creative director, Chris Payne, who then offered her a job as a designer. A year later the studio merged with a design and advertising agency, and then became affiliated with an international partner to form TBWA/ CREATIVE.

According to Bharij, much design in Kenya is informed by the geography, wildlife, plants, colours and heterogeneous culture of the country. She points out that Kenya has more than forty different tribes, including the Masai, Samburu and Swahili. "We work with such a diverse clientele," she says, "so work ranges from low-budget design to jobs for clients who will pay top-dollar. What I do find in Kenya, however, is that people in general, and clients, need to be more open to ideas. A lot of the time great ideas and designs are shot down because clients think they're too clever for the market and are afraid to take risks. But in this way they don't give the market a chance to react, or to decide what to make of an idea. How are we meant to move forward if everyone just sticks to the same principles, ways and ideas? That's my question!"

One example of a low-budget project undertaken by Bharij was the design of a brochure for Savage Paradise, a company that operates safari tours in Kenya and one of its bordering countries, Tanzania. "The brief was to design something within a limited budget but eye-catching," she explains. "That's where the use of the vibrant colours and the background images come into it. The colours relate to the great African sunsets, the landscapes, and the clothes and jewellery worn by the Masai, a celebrated tribe that could be said to symbolize the great Kenyan and Tanzanian landscapes."

In another project, Bharij designed a calendar for Delmonte Kenya Ltd, a Nairobi-based company that manufactures and packages tinned fruit and juices. The brief was to create a link between the company's products and people. "I came up with the idea of using the tins as pieces of jewellery, so the theme was 'Delmonte Adorned'," she says. "In this way I also had the opportunity to depict different aspects of the culture in Kenya, including dance, movement, dress and jewellery."

"A lot of the time great ideas and designs are shot down because clients think they're too clever for the market and are afraid to take risks." AJMEET BHARIJ

## Last year, we had a million visitors. Were you one of them?

Each year, over 950,000 visitors from all over the world make Nigeria their vacation destination. Where do they go, what do they see or do? The answer is easy, when you consider that Nigeria has forrest reserves where you can see wildlife, warm springs where you can float around and relax, crafts markets to browse and hundreds of unique local festivals you cannot see any where else. You can stay at one of the many five-star hotels, or enjoy local sights from your window in an African hut. In the evening, dance to the latest tunes at a popular bar, or have a moonlight dinner by the Atlantic Ocean.

To learn more about Nigerian vacations, go to **www.visitnigeria.com**, or call your local travel agent.

## NIGERIA
*One country, 10,000 destinations and a whole lot of friendly people!*

## Are you headed for the same destination again this year?

**120 million people and 10,000 destinations,** national parks and forrest reserves, warm springs and local crafts markets, hundreds of unique local festivals you cannot see any where else. You are welcome to stay at a secure five-star hotels, or enjoy local sights from your window in an African hut. In the evenings, feel the rhythm at a popular bar, or have dinner by moonlight beach.

To learn more about Nigerian vacations, go to **www.visitnigeria.com**, or call your local travel agent.

## NIGERIA
*One country, 10,000 destinations and a whole lot of friendly people!*

## Desert Taxi.

## NIGERIA
*One country, 10,000 destinations and a whole lot of friendly people!*

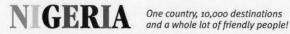

## Dance Party.

**120 million people and thousands of distinct tribal groups,** you would never tire of hearing new sounds or getting down to different music each night. Feel the deep, African rhythms at a popular bar, or dance the night away at the village square, with music from gourds, gongs, agogos and *gon-gon's*. Your friends back home will not believe what you did last night. It's no wonder they say the night is alive in Nigeria.

To learn more about Nigerian vacations, go to **www.visitnigeria.com**, or call your local travel agent.

## NIGERIA
*One country, 10,000 destinations and a whole lot of friendly people!*

'SEGUN OLUDE GRADUATED from the School of Art, Printing and Design at Yaba College of Technology in Lagos, Nigeria, and then completed a major in Graphic Design with honours at the University of Manitoba in Canada.

Olude feels that he has benefited from his experience and knowledge of both Nigerian and Western cultures. "Patterns and symbols from both worlds become very important elements," he says, "and my current fascination is with the use and meanings of symbols in different cultures. The characteristics of my native language, Yoruba, have always made me want to simplify long metaphors into very short, simple visual messages, to avoid double meaning. Everything must be clear and immediate, especially when it comes to informational posters and public promotions. Another cultural influence from Nigeria is the use of vibrant colours, and I find myself often embracing this use of strong, bright tones."

The prevailing economic circumstances in Nigeria have had a strong influence on all aspects of life in the country, including graphic design, as Olude explains: "Our resources have been depleted in recent years, and people use what they can find. It is not uncommon to find graphic designers getting colour separation done on a greyscale laser printer. You can imagine what the final outcome will be!

Most designers in Nigeria are trying so hard to imitate the West that we have lost a bit of ground in our own traditional forms of visual expression."

One design project undertaken by Olude in 2001 was the development of an advertising campaign to raise awareness of Nigeria as a tourist destination. First he set about finding out what 'Nigeria' signifies to a foreigner, and how a number of myths and fears about travel in Nigeria might be dispelled. He used photographs to tell the story and convey the message, and was careful to let the design play a secondary role to the photographs, an approach that he believes gave more credibility to the campaign.

"Most designers in Nigeria are trying so hard to imitate the West that we have lost a bit of ground in our own traditional forms of visual expression." 'SEGUN OLUDE

The road less travelled.

If we told you our story of all the wonderful things you will see or do in Nigeria, perhaps you'd believe us. But we thought we would let this photograph by a real tourist, speak for itself. Yes, this is Nigeria, and this is the kind of sight that awaits you, when you make Nigeria your next vacation destination.

Come enjoy year-round sunshine. Come for the thrill of the night clubs. Spend the night in an African hut, if that's what you like to do. You may even visit the many museums and art galleries in the major cities. Whatever you like to do, we probably have. Even if all you want is just sunshine. Call your travel agent today, or visit us on the web at www.visitnigeria.com, to get off the beaten paths.

**NIGERIA**
*One country, 10,000 destinations
a whole lot of friendly people!*

THE THREE-YEAR COURSE IN Graphic Design taken by Roy Clucas at Natal Technical College in the 1960s was interrupted by nine months of compulsory military training. While in the army he practised signwriting, and after a brief and successful stint at this following graduation he applied for a job with an advertising agency. He remembers that his "largely psychedelic art-school portfolio" was deemed by the creative director to be inadequate, but he was offered a job as an account executive. Within a year he had "wangled a spot" in the studio, working on such major tasks as the design of an exhibition stand for an automotive group. A few months afterwards he accepted a job as a designer at a group called PIG.

"Thirty odd years later," he says, "after a career journey that has led to my working in New York, Paris and Cape Town, and allowed me to travel to the East, South America and Australia, all the while remaining a student and willing slave of design, I'm still doing it. That design project thing. Mostly in the guise of a 'creative director' who still calls Joburg home."

Clucas names many "influential heroes", who span artistic, scientific and cultural realms. He is fascinated by creative architecture, furniture and product design, has always enjoyed the links between Art Deco and African arts and crafts,

and follows car design "like a groupie". He points out that he is not a huge fan of nationalistic or societal territorialism, and favours an eclectic approach to design: "There is much that is distinctive about our indigenous visual imagery, and one is consistently thrilled by the delights of naïve expression that emanate from an emerging country such as ours. Appreciating the importance of humour and spontaneity to design acceptance is an ongoing interest and endeavour. But one is also acutely aware that something too oft repeated can become clichéd – an embarrassment to the more worldly observer."

The conceptualization and execution of a calendar for the paper company Sappi in 2001 proved to be a very satisfying project for Clucas, particularly because he collaborated with other designers and specialists. The calendar became the recipient of a Sappi 'Ideas that Matter' grant. According to Clucas: "In an environment where so few truly conceptual pieces reach fruition because of the fixation with traditional imagery, this one – despite various compromises – is one that still satisfies when I see it, which is every day in our studio!"

1  Book cover, slip case and typography for a retrospective on the South African artist Norman Catherine, 2000
2  Calendar cover for the paper manufacturer Sappi, 2001
3  Logo/mascot for a website and retail network selling South African crafts, 1997
4  One of a series of four posters on canvas board, promoting jazz concerts sponsored by a local brewery, 1986
5  Proposal for a new national symbol for South Africa, 1999

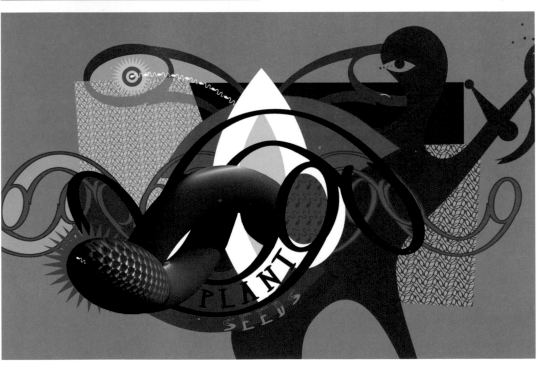

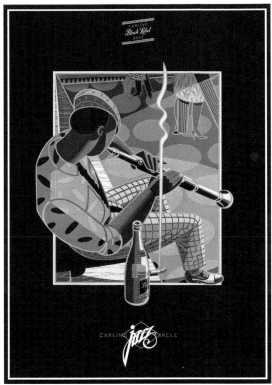

"There is much that is distinctive about our indigenous visual imagery, and one is consistently thrilled by the delights of naïve expression that emanate from an emerging country such as ours."
ROY CLUCAS

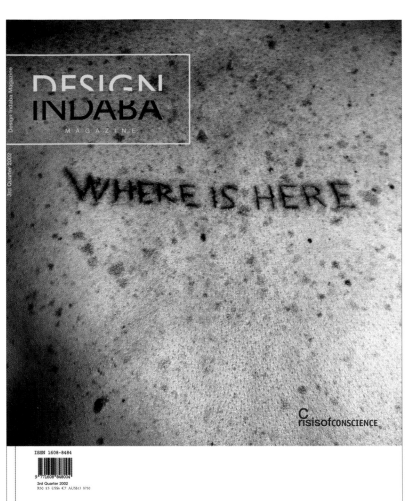

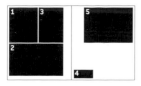

1 Cover for the quarterly magazine *Design Indaba*, 2002
2 Double-page spread for *Design Indaba* magazine, 2001
3 Poster for the 'Hip2b²' project, 2002
4 Logo for South African Airways, 1996
5 Media promotion for the 'First African in Space' project, 2002

There's only one thing that could stop the University of Port Elizabeth's Dr Vaughan Oosthuizen from a possible breakthrough in solving protein structures.

O NOTHING

First African in Space

www.africaninspace.com

Just think. What if superior-quality protein crystals could possibly be grown under zero-gravity conditions? What if the only barrier between us and solving protein structures was the Earth's atmosphere? What if these crystals could bring us one step closer to solving the structure of the proteins involved in allergies and HIV infection? Here in Africa, we're not scared to ask 'what if...?' We're not scared to dream. When we got the opportunity to conduct experiments on the International Space Station, South African science stepped boldly forward. At most, the results will teach us invaluable information in the field of drug research. At the very least, it will teach us to keep asking, 'what if...?' And to remember to let nothing stand in our way. Cutting-edge biotechnology won't just save lives in Africa, it could put us ahead in the commercial race too. Which is why HBD Venture Capital invests in the best South African biotech ideas. Nothing Ventured, Nothing Gained.

Vaughan Oosthuizen - Biochemist

HBD

"American popular culture and television dominated our living-rooms in the 1980s ... I've kept these influences with me and used them in my approach to design. Thinking locally and acting globally!"

MICHAEL STALLENBERG

"BEING SOUTH AFRICAN MEANS that one's life is bombarded by politics, whether you like it or not," says graphic designer Michael Stallenberg. "Growing up as a teenager in the 1980s was a visual thrill for me. From the 'Free Mandela' posters to the boycotts and toyi-toying, to 'European Only' signs, to police capers everywhere you looked, I was bombarded with visual language.

"Although our families struggled financially, it didn't stop people in our neighbourhood sporting the latest brands. You were identified in terms of your area and status by your Converse sneakers, your London Fog jacket, or your Lee denims. Through this and my love for football I was introduced to the power of brands: Puma, Kappa, Adidas, Umbro, Diadora, Lotto and Le Coq Sportif almost defined our teenage years. American popular culture and television dominated our living-rooms in the 1980s, and magazines from Europe and America became our window to the world. I fell in love with movie posters and used to remove them from lamp-posts and even cinemas. I've kept these influences with me and used them in my approach to design. Thinking locally and acting globally!"

Stallenberg completed a graphic-design course at Port Elizabeth Technikon in 1994, going on to work in various studios before joining the Capetown-based company Interactive Africa in 2000. He joined mainly

to work on the quarterly magazine *Design Indaba*, which has been developed to accompany the annual International Design Indaba event. The magazine showcases African and subcontinental design, and includes articles from such notables as the typographer and author Lewis Blackwell to keep readers abreast of international design trends and theories.

Two of Stallenberg's most memorable design projects were based on the 'First African in Space' campaign in 2002. He designed a media insert for Mark Shuttleworth's mission that contained information on the scientific research programme and created awareness of the opportunities for South African space research. A related project was the media campaign for the project 'Hip2b²', which was aimed at inspiring South African youth, in the wake of the 'First African in Space' project, to focus on maths and science studies using their own esoteric and abbreviated language.

"We are telling schoolkids across the continent that, in case they haven't noticed, it has become hip to be square," says Stallenberg. "To illustrate this fusion of hip and square, the campaign marries visuals of 'uncool or square' items with visuals of 'hip and happening' people and situations. Clark Kent glasses are now de rigueur."

SOUTH AFRICAN AIRWAYS

GARTH WALKER

# BLACK APOLLO

# PLUMBERS BUTT

GARTH WALKER TRAINED AS a graphic designer in Durban in the 1970s. He started Orange Juice Design in 1995, and since at first he had no work and no clients, he created OJ's studio magazine *i-jusi* (Zulu for 'juice') with the objective of "promoting and encouraging a local design language rooted in the South African experience". Walker has since accumulated a large collection of African vernacular design imagery, and is in the process of producing a book and a TV game show. His work has been recognized with more than sixty local and international awards.

"Although we have a rich visual tradition in South Africa," says Walker, "we don't have a tradition of graphic design, only craft. That's why we have an opportunity to do something unique, as we don't have to undo anything. So let's use this visual tradition to begin a new design language that everybody can understand: one that mixes icons from the past and borrows from different cultures; a visual language that draws on the visual imagery of the stuff around us and incorporates spoken and written language (bearing in mind that we have eleven official languages)."

Walker points out that the election in May 1994, when Nelson Mandela became the first democratically elected president of South Africa, not only marked the crossover into a new South Africa but also heralded a new way of seeing. "From that day we had the freedom to redefine ourselves, to feel renewed in the present, to be revitalized in the future," he says. "Our visual language is our most powerful weapon. It's our tool of change. The South African creative spirit has always had the power to bring together all the powers that be – be they violent, political, racial, healing, spiritual, individual or national – and lay them on a page in front of us."

At a conference held in Zurich in 1999 entitled 'Towards-transit: new visual languages in South Africa', Walker presented a paper called 'Shoe Repairs Here: graphic design from the streets and townships of South Africa'. Accompanied by a visual presentation, it argued that street graphics reflect the process of transition in South Africa. The influence of African countries to the north has always been apparent in street graphics, but new regional designs and symbols are beginning to emerge. This is apparent in the transient but increasingly sophisticated painted signs, murals and hoardings for shoe repairers, hair salons, buses and taxis. "Indigenous South Africans love special effects in their visual language," says Walker. "From clothing to type, from pictorial images to cars, from houses to sunglasses, all have an excess about them. It is all very nouveau riche really!"

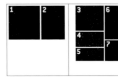

1  Black Apollo typeface designed as a spoof on 1970s cosmetic packaging, 2001
2  Vernacular typeface, a spoof on a plumber's sign found on a Durban street, 2002
3  A poster series promoting South African consumer-packaging graphics, for an international printmaking conference held in Cape Town, 2003
4  Cover and double-page spread for an issue of *i-jusi* magazine on African death culture, 1996
5  Cover and double-page spread for an issue of *i-jusi* magazine on African design language, 1996
6  Covers for the first four issues of the experimental graphic-design magazine *i-jusi*, 1996
7  CD cover designed to interpret new African jazz sounds for a Swiss music publisher, 1997

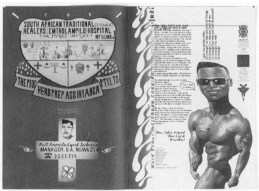

"Our visual language is our most powerful weapon. It's our tool of change." GARTH WALKER

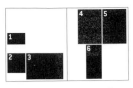

1 Label/package design for a condiment manufacturer, 2002
2 CD cover for Managing African Design Evolvement (MADE), 2001
3 Brand design for use on billboards, 2000
4 Cover design for *huru* magazine, 2003
5 Page design for *huru* magazine, for an article on the Zimbabwean painter and sculptor Wayne Stutchbury, 2003
6 Brand design for a salon offering African aromatherapy, 2003

**MICHAEL DANES COMPLETED** a three-year City & Guilds Design for Print course in Harare in the mid-1980s, and since that time he has been working as a graphic designer. "I started Danes Design in Harare in 1992," he says, "and I spend most of my time rearing new designers, teaching clients the purpose of design, and struggling to sustain the company in a strange economic/political environment." The work of Danes Design is focused on branding, packaging, publication, corporate identity, interior retail and website design. An ongoing objective of the studio is "purposefully to challenge the perception of African design and to brand African products innovatively for every market – Zimbabwean, regional and international".

Danes nominates as an important influence on his design approach the Zimbabwean designer Chaz Maviyane-Davies, whose work on human rights issues, he believes, has described a new culture in African graphic design. He has been impressed also by the innovative film, video and photography of Tom Roope, Director of Tomato Interactive UK, and by British designer Neville Brody of *Fetish*, *The Face* and *Arena* fame. "My work is influenced also by the natural landscape of Zimbabwe, which is a wild country with vast national parks," he adds. "We visit these frequently, and I would have to say that nature informs most of my work."

In 2003 Mike Danes designed *huru* magazine, a publication intended for distribution in his region of Zimbabwe. According to Danes: "The aim of the publication is to try to uplift Zimbabweans' perception of their country in the midst of all the current political hardship. The publishers have tried to achieve this through the use of photography of everyday street scenes and simple interviews with common people." Another project, in 2002, was the design of a new brand label for Elephant Pepper chilli products, which are manufactured in Zimbabwe from raw materials collected from local farmers. "The concept of the brand comes from the threat to the crops of local farmers from elephants raiding their fields. When the farmers grow chilli bushes around the boundary of the field the elephants are warded off because of a fear that animals have of chilli."

Danes has also completed a rebranding and packaging project for Nature Nurture, manufacturers of aromatherapy products made from local herbs. "The client requested the rebranding exercise to increase regional sales of its products," he says. "I introduced African-made textures and masks on the packaging and corporate stationery to enhance the notion of dark African intrigue."

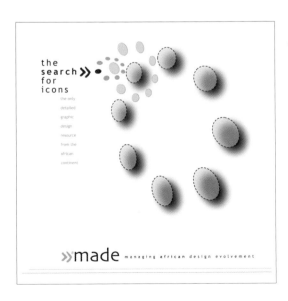

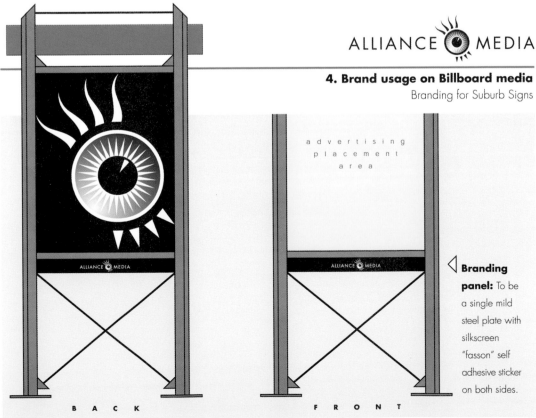

**4. Brand usage on Billboard media**
Branding for Suburb Signs

advertising placement area

BACK

FRONT

◁ **Branding panel:** To be a single mild steel plate with silkscreen "fasson" self adhesive sticker on both sides.

**BIG**
lifestyles
socials
feelings
cultures

# huru

No.1 March 2003

cellphone card sellers

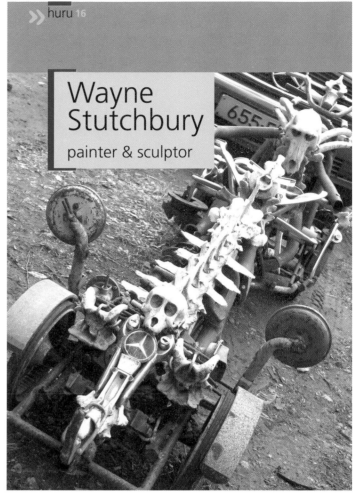

## Wayne Stutchbury
painter & sculptor

"My work is influenced also by the natural landscape of Zimbabwe, which is a wild country with vast national parks. We visit these frequently, and I would have to say that nature informs most of my work." MICHAEL DANES

8 Martin Drive, Msasa, PO Box AY 359 Amby, Harare, Zimbabwe. Tel: (263-4) 487833/496754. Fax: (263-4) 496753. **Email:** naturenurture@com www.naturenurture@com

[*nature*]
nurture

**AFRICAN** AROMA THERAPY

SAKI MAFUNDIKWA

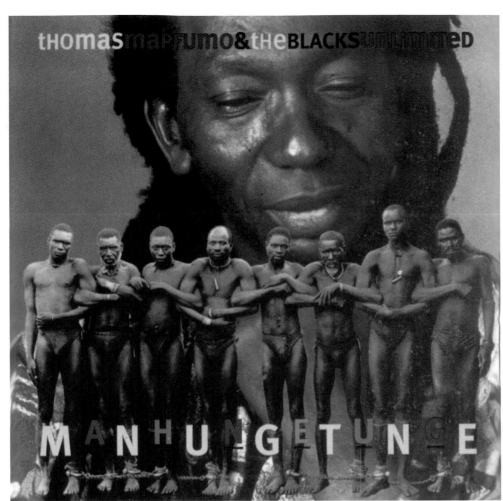

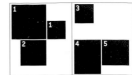

1 CD covers for the group Thomas
Mapfumo and the Blacks Unlimited,
2001
2 Album cover for the group Thomas
Mapfumo and the Blacks Unlimited,
1989
3 Brochure for UNDP (United Nations
Development Programme) Africa,
1999
4 Logo for the Black Documentary
Collective, New York, 2002
5 Logo for the 4th Zimbabwe
International Film Festival, 2001

"The masks that blew Picasso's
mind and led to his creation of
Cubism, which led in turn to the
creation of graphic design, came
from Africa." SAKI MAFUNDIKWA

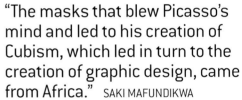

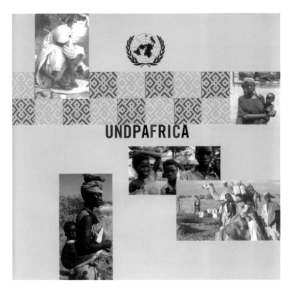

UNDPAFRICA

SAKI MAFUNDIKWA IS THE Director of ZIVA, the Zimbabwe Institute of Vigital Arts, which he founded in 1997. After his early education in Zimbabwe he studied Telecommunications and Fine Arts at Indiana University before completing his MFA in Graphic Design at Yale. During Mafundikwa's years of education in the United States his work was influenced by "Modernists totally immersed in the Swiss style", including Paul Rand, Herbert Matter, Armin Hoffman and Bradbury Thompson, and he feels fortunate to have studied under some of these leading figures.

"It was only when I left college that I started to question the relevance of an African with a Swiss-looking portfolio. I decided to let the real Saki stand up, and I began to make a conscious effort to let my work reflect who I was: an African. Most of the vision for ZIVA was born around this time. It was to be an African Bauhaus, where new ideas in visual communication could be hatched."

Mafundikwa has no doubt about what should characterize the graphic design that emanates from his country and region. "Colours, colours, colours," he emphasizes. "Mention Africa to most people in other parts of the world and the words they say come to mind are sun, heat, nature, friendly, organic, human, developing, ethnic, strife, art, music *etc.* I do not deal just with my country, I deal with my continent. Graphic design, after all, originated in Africa. The masks that blew Picasso's mind and led to his creation of Cubism, which led in turn to the creation of graphic design, came from Africa. So this is the source of it all, and the design we are trying to create at ZIVA will be of, from and about Africa."

A project that reflects this approach was Mafundikwa's design in 2001 of the logo for the 4th Zimbabwe International Film Festival (ZIFF), held in Harare. Mafundikwa says that he had been overlooked as the designer in previous years because his work was considered to be "too African", and not sufficiently international. However, a new director of ZIFF commissioned Mafundikwa to design a logo that combined "African" feeling with international appeal. "I decided to go for a typographic solution," says Saki, "creating the ZIFF logotype using geometric shapes found in southern African art. I drew on Ndebele art, as I often do. The client was ecstatic with the solution, and the logo received praise from visiting international film-makers."

BLACK DOCUMENTARY COLLECTIVE

ZIMBABWE INTERNATIONAL FILM FESTIVAL TRUST
26 Cork Road
PO Box A4
Avondale
Harare Zimbabwe

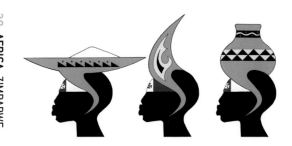

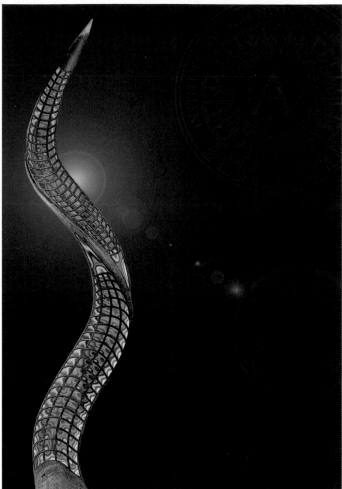

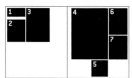

1   Christmas card for the British Council based on 'Three Wise Women', 1992
2   *Everyone has the right to take part in the government of his country, directly or through freely chosen representatives,* a poster from a series on the United Nations Articles on Human Rights, based on Article 21, 1996
3   Poster for the Institute of Architects of Zimbabwe (IAZ) for an exhibition of contemporary architecture, 2000
4   Cover for a political magazine published after the 1985 elections in Zimbabwe, 1985
5   CD cover for the jazz band Mapapiro ('Little Wing'), 2000
6   Poster for an exhibiton of Zimbabwean rock painting, 1999
7   *No one should be subjected to slavery or servitude,* a poster from a series based on the United Nations Articles on Human Rights, 1996

CHAZ MAVIYANE-DAVIES HAD an unorthodox introduction to a career in graphic design, starting out as a trainee draughtsman for the local telecommunications corporation in Zimbabwe. While there, he was asked to work on a design project because he had some drawing skills and the organization was unwilling to pay for a professional designer. After demonstrating to himself and others that he had some talent, he determined to train as a graphic designer.

At this time, in the early 1970s, Maviyane-Davies felt that discriminatory policies in Zimbabwe would prevent him from pursuing his interest in design, and as a result, he undertook his graphic-design studies first in neighbouring Zambia and then in England, finishing with an MA from the Central School of Art and Design in London. After graduating he returned to Zimbabwe to practise, first as principal in a sizeable graphic-design company and later, when the corporate life became unsatisfying to him personally, in a one-person studio.

"My destiny as an African designer is bound up with the necessity for profound social change," says Maviyane-Davies. "Graphic design must strive to communicate the extent of misery, illiteracy and injustice through exploitation, and must not be thwarted at the outset. Growing up with discrimination has given me the resolve to fight this virus using whatever talents I have at my disposal."

The majority of Maviyane-Davies's work involves cultural and humanitarian projects that he selects as suitable. The work covers corporate identity, book and magazine design, posters, annual reports and show-stand design. "My curiosity", he says, "comes from my fascination with people, politics and culture. These are the focal points of my work and imagination. I believe in working with surreal notions about life to make my work more expressive. Film, which I studied as a postgraduate student at Central St Martin's College of Art and Design in London, offers the added narrative of motion and sound."

Maviyane-Davies describes graphic design as "the commercial derivative of art for communication", and points out that this is a new phenomenon from which indigenous Africans have been excluded until recently. "Sadly, apart from imitation, we seem at present limited to appropriating traditional African iconography as a cosmetic hard sell, without investing in the vibrancy and vitality from which it came. While there are a few examples of work from designers who are attempting to break away from that tendency, very little of it resonates and emerges into clear bodies of work."

# MOTO

AUGUST 1985
No 37

50 cents (including sales tax)

**Election aftermath**

"Graphic design must strive to communicate the extent of misery, illiteracy and injustice through exploitation, and must not be thwarted at the outset."

CHAZ MAVIYANE-DAVIES

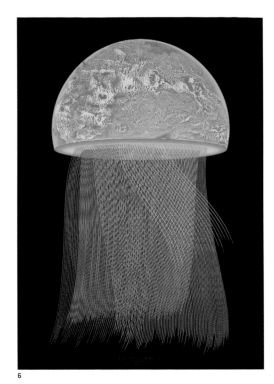

6

森羅万象　横尾忠則

ART

TADANORI YOKOO 2002·8·10→10·27

M0+
MUSEUM CONTEMPORARY TOKYO OF ART
東京都現代美術館

7

Sudarshan Dheer supports this view, arguing that the visual-communication environment in India is dominated by the advertising agencies, while Shankar Barua believes that Indian graphic designers must continue to look to the villages of India for distinctively Indian colours and visual icons. In Barry Dawson's book *Street Graphics India* (1999), his visual examples demonstrate vividly the power of vernacular graphics on hoardings, street furniture, vehicles, buildings and packaging. "Striking images [on political, religious and commercial themes] blur in a confusion of colour, scale and quantity," he says. "Images are individually crafted by street artists, with particular and regional variations in style and technique." Dawson explains that most of the street graphics are not produced with the uniformity of computer-aided design or lithographic printing, but are hand-rendered. Trucks, buses and rickshaws are transformed into kinetic art, personalized with symbols and motifs of religious and natural imagery.

The graphic design profession in Singapore benefited considerably from the industrial prosperity of the South East Asian region during the 1980s. The economic boom created an increased demand for advertising and corporate-identity design, particularly in the information technology sector. In 1988 the Singapore Trade Development Board (TDB) and the International Design Forum Singapore (IDF) began jointly to promote international design conferences,

competitions and industry events, and the Designers Association Singapore (DAS) is now a joint organizer of the Singapore Design Award and the Asian Young Designers Award. A number of magazines that feature contemporary design, and demonstrate high standards of layout, typography, illustration and photography, are now published in Singapore. These include *Nuyou*, *Female*, *Torque* and *SilverKris*.

In 2001 the Designers Association Singapore and Hypersummer Matters co-published the first edition of *designer*, a quarterly magazine that aims "to be a vehicle for serious discussion about design and what concerns designers in Singapore, Asia and the world as a whole". In an article in the first issue, entitled 'In Search of Singapore Design', the editor looked for "the subtle influences that make a design uniquely Singaporean". Some of the sources of influence suggested in the article, including cultural heritage, faces, sunshine and bright colours, could apply to numerous other countries and regions, but one idea seemed to have particular relevance for Singapore and the South East Asian region: "Local designers learn to draw with both brush and pencil – one foot in the East and one in the West. ... A bilingual friend once told me that if he wanted to solve a logical problem he would think in English, but if he wanted to think around it more laterally he would change to thinking in Chinese. This is a unique quality that many Singaporean designers have, and this can be a

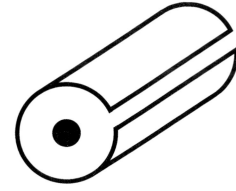

**TheWooRing E&P**

9

**Haein-sa Museum Opening**
2002年 7月 5日 (佛紀 2546年 7月 5日)
海印寺聖寶博物館

8

valuable bridge between cultures as the Asian economy continues to emerge."

The design culture in other South East Asian countries is not as developed as in Singapore, owing to a range of religious, cultural, political and economic factors. The predominance of Islam in Malaysia and Indonesia, and of Buddhism in Laos and Vietnam, has contributed to some resistance in these countries to Western consumerist values, and this has affected the development of graphic design. International advertising agencies were attracted to Kuala Lumpur in Malaysia during the boom economic period of the 1980s, and most graphic design work for the corporate world has been undertaken by their creative departments. There are still very few design studios in the country.

Of all South East Asian countries, Laos presents the most extreme example of how conflict and adherence to traditional beliefs can affect the development of a design culture. As a result of the conflicts in the region during the 1970s, Laos has the dubious distinction of being the most heavily bombed nation on earth in terms of bombs per capita. During the 1975 revolution, 10% of its middle-class citizens fled the country, and another 40,000 were imprisoned. At this time, Laos was not self-sufficient in rice, and despite some industrial growth in the past thirty years it is still among the world's least developed countries. Following the

1975 revolution, the new government imposed tight regulations on a range of activities in order to hasten a return to Laotian Buddhist traditions. These regulations, many of which are still in place, affected Laotian dress, hairstyles, entertainment, food and music, and continue to have an impact on design developments. Local industry and trade have been advanced to the extent that there are now some opportunities for graphic designers, but, according to an estimate by the president of Icograda in 2002, there were then fewer than ten practising designers in Laos, and only a few of these were graphic designers.

Across the Mekong River, in Thailand, there are fewer indications of design development being retarded by religious or cultural beliefs. While industrial growth in Thailand has undergone a recession following the boom of the 1980s, the entertainment industry in Thailand is thriving, and this is creating increasing work for graphic designers. It varies from posters and graphics for Thai films, some of which have won awards at international film festivals, to brash commercials for Thai television, to seductive promotions for Thailand's more exotic attractions. As in most Asian countries, attempts to retain religious and cultural traditions and to resist Western consumerism are being countered by the power of global communications, particularly that of the Internet.

我仍然相信    I still Believe

10

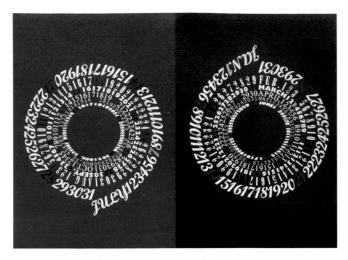

1 Calendar card for a printing company
  (front and back), 1995
2 Recruitment poster for Shantou
  University, 1997
3 *Victory*, a silkscreen poster, 1998
4 *Transformation* playing-card design,
  1988–2001
5 *Victim*, a graphic artwork for the 2nd
  Internet Graphic Design Competition,
  1988

## FANG CHEN

 FANG CHEN IS PROFESSOR OF Graphic Design at Wuhan University of Technology in China, and Visiting Artist at both The Cooper Union School of Art in New York and The University of Texas at Austin. Born in Wuhan, in Hubei Province, he received his Bachelor of Science in Graphic Design from Hubei Institute of Technology and his MFA from Hubei Academy of Fine Arts.

Chen has written extensively about graphic design and design education, including a series of books entitled 'The World Masters', showcasing international designers. His work has been reproduced widely, for example in *Graphis*, *Novum*, *Print*, *Etapes graphiques*, *Communication Arts*, *Idea* and UNESCO's *Courier*. He is the recipient of many international awards, including four gold medals in design competitions in Asia, Europe and the United States.

"In my opinion, the idea is the soul of graphic design," says Chen. "And the creation of the idea is the result of cumulative knowledge and broad artistic immersion. With regard to poster design, I think that explaining the profound in simple terms is very important." In his poster *Victory*, designed in 1998, he first used silkscreen printing, and after repeating the work using photography he completed an associated piece entitled *Victim*.

"Both *Victory* and *Victim* are based on 'the hand', as many renowned Chinese artworks, both ancient and modern, treat the hand. Artworks should be the result of philosophical ideas, and I used black and white to represent, respectively, the yin and yang of traditional Chinese philosophy. The capital 'v' is a universal symbol for victory that is understood by viewers from all races and cultures. According to Chinese folklore, the lines in human hands not only record the past but also foretell the future. In my image I wanted the palm lines in the hand to show that human beings of all periods often go through numerous struggles and sufferings in order to survive and ultimately triumph. Through the missing three fingers, I intended to extend the feeling of victimization in the image and, at the same time, to add to the poster's theatrical effect."

Chen's design for a pack of playing cards was inspired by the Figure Cards of Heroes of the Water Margin Chronicles by the seventeenth-century painter Lao-lian Chen. Fang Chen designed a pack of double-faced cards based on a principle of illusion that would be an extension of the double-ended Western pattern: "The heads of each subject are derived from Chinese history or mythology, and the key feature of the design is the illustration of two moods for each subject. For example, the king is a portrait of Gongming Zhao, who was known as the Spirit of Wealth and reportedly was able to summon thunder and lightning, eradicate evil and epidemics, uphold justice and deliver riches."

> "The idea is the soul of graphic design." FANG CHEN

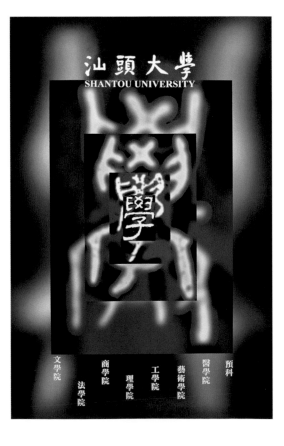

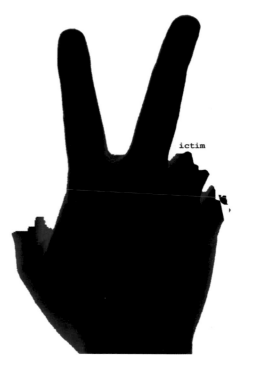

ictim

WANG XU

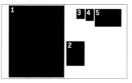

1 Cover of a New Members' Report for the Alliance Graphique Internationale, 2001
2 *Paper*, a poster for the Taiwan Poster Design Association, 2001
3 Cover of a calendar for Airbus Industries, 2001
4 Poster for the book *Artistic Conception Writing*, 2000
5 Double-page spread in the book *Artistic Conception Writing*, 2000

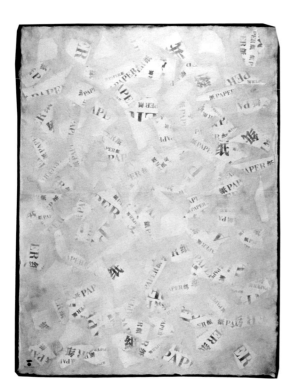

WANG XU BELIEVES THAT IT is important to reflect the Chinese character and culture in his graphic design. "I could not design well if I did not have a good understanding of both," he says. "In capturing the Chinese character in my designs I usually adopt two modes of thinking. First, if I am depicting a particular person in a poster or book jacket, I search for the deep meaning inside the character. Second, I sometimes try to internationalize the Chinese character, to give it an international image that can be understood by people who don't know the Chinese culture well."

Xu studied graphic design at the Guangzhou Academy of Fine Arts in the 1970s, and began his practice at the China Packaging Import & Export (Guangdong) Company. He worked on packaging design for food exports, and points out that in those days it was not common for English to be used on export packaging. Following the open-door policy adopted by China in the early 1980s, Chinese design became increasingly influenced by Western trends. It was a particular challenge at that time, Xu remembers, to adopt a new approach to packaging design for Western markets.

In the decades since then, Wang Xu has earned an international reputation for his design of posters, publications and numerous other graphic forms. Among his favourite projects was his design of a poster entitled *Paper* for the 2001 exhibition of the Taiwan Poster Design Association. The poster was inspired by a Taiwanese man's dream of establishing a handmade-paper workshop to ensure the continuation of the original papermaking technique – one of China's four major inventions. When he was tragically killed in a plane crash, his daughter carried on the dream. Xu had visited her workshop years before and remembered her story.

"My idea for the poster was quite simple," says Xu. "First I printed the word 'paper' in complex and simplified Chinese, and in English, on some pieces of paper. The reason for the mix of Chinese characters was that Taiwan uses complex Chinese and the mainland uses simplified Chinese. When the papers were printed I tore them into small pieces and spread them in the paper pulp to form the poster."

"I sometimes try to internationalize the Chinese character, to give it an international image that can be understood by people who don't know the Chinese culture well."

WANG XU

SHANKAR BARUA DESCRIBES himself as "primarily a designer/creator of tiny little impellers and footnotes to the creative history of my era and circumstances". Based in Delhi, he follows several different creative avenues in pursuit of this end, both professionally and personally – imaging, writing, photography, music and "basic-video, basic-html, basic event-management".

Barua's professional development has been informed by numerous experiences, including studies in art and journalism, and professional work as an advertising copywriter, a tea executive and taster, an editor and a musician. He spent the 1980s as an adventure-travel writer and photographer, venturing off the beaten track throughout western India, northeast India and the northern Himalayas. He is therefore also strongly aware of issues of population size and density, empowerment, the environment and natural justice. Among international influences he nominates Alphonse Mucha: "The Moravian artist Alphonse Mucha has been a big inspiration to me, on the basis of the seventy-two plates of his 'Documents Decoratifs'. I even use a serpent from the book alongside my name on some of my projects."

To Barua, there are two very different faces and personalities to India, an urban and a rural India, each also reflecting a different approach to visual imagery and graphic design. "Design in Indian cities is increasingly global," he says, "but rural India is, to me, more clearly *Indian*. In the villages, I tend to see a love for rich, pure, even loud colours, sometimes with traditional local favourites. We find also an associated love for shiny things, the whole business of patterns popping up everywhere, the guileless acceptance and embracing of elementary visual icons." He likes to think that this is demonstrated most prominently in Hindi cinema, but it is certainly also reflected and developed in other media and advertising that target rural India.

Since the year 2000 the project that has been occupying Barua's mind is 'The IDEA' ('The Indian Documentary of Electronic Arts'), a six-monthly series of CD-gazettes that seeks to address all forms of Computer-Based Creative Practice (CBCP) ranging from imaging through audio, video, design and 3D, even to arts at present inconceivable. Among the primary inspirations behind this project is the perception that with real-world space rapidly shrinking, especially in such countries as India, virtual space can provide an escape hatch for many creative activities. "It's the biggest and wildest card I've ever played," he says, "and it has turned up trumps for me and for the numerous artists who have participated in many different ways."

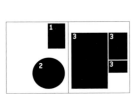

1  Promotional photograph/calligraphy
   for the Indian pharmaceutical
   company CIPLA, 2001
2  CD cover for 'The IDEA' (The Indian
   Documentary of Electronic Arts), 2001
3  Gazette covers for 'The IDEA', 2002,
   2002, 2001

"Design in Indian cities is increasingly global, but rural India is, to me, more clearly *Indian*."
SHANKAR BARUA

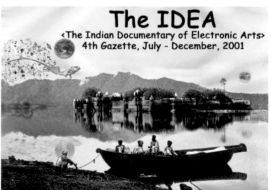

ITU CHAUDHURI

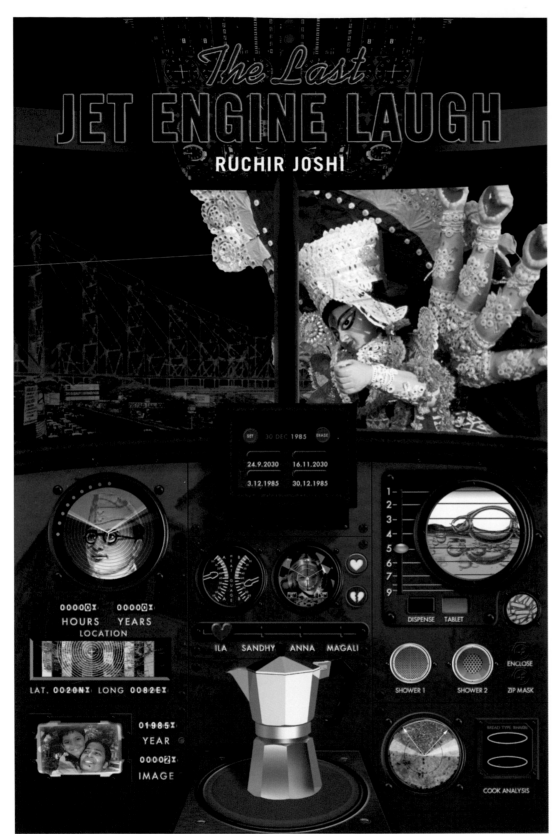

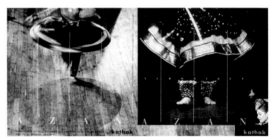

EAST WEST

# INDIGO

ITU CHAUDHURI STUDIED architecture in India in the early 1980s before concentrating on graphic design. As design practices were uncommon in India at the time, he worked on his own, sometimes as an itinerant designer and later from home under the name Itu Chaudhuri Design (ICD). He set up a fully fledged company and office in New Delhi in 1996.

Chaudhuri believes that his approach to design was influenced significantly by his meeting with the famed Indian designer Aurobind Patel in 1984. "My interest in type and lettering brought us together," he explains. "He was the most important influence during those formative years when you set your compass and acquire a set of design values/touchstones that tell you what is worth doing.

"But the factor that has had the biggest influence on my approach has been the design vacuum in India. This is a country with just one real design school, the National Institute of Design in Ahmedabad, and it was only when students from NID began to work with me that I was able to discuss design with the vocabulary and concepts I possessed. Obviously I have learnt a lot through this process. Responding to a market and making a living from design takes a much heavier toll of a designer in a developing country. The tone and text(ure) of the concerns voiced by Western designers would seem comically utopian in India."

Chaudhuri feels that, as India globalizes, its designers will become increasingly international in their values and concerns. The exceptions, he says, will be those designers who use traditional Indian imagery/iconography as kitsch or for ironic or self-reflective humour. As an example he cites, somewhat disparagingly, the tendency of Western publishers producing books by Indian authors in English to have these covers scream 'India' as loudly as possible. "ICD covers", he says, "have a more international sensibility, as Indian writing in English has its own place in the world, and confining its representation to images of Indian silk or Indian spices is condescending, or annoyingly Orientalist."

In a cover designed recently for the novel *The Last Jet Engine Laugh* by Ruchir Joshi, Chaudhuri used the metaphor of a jet dashboard for the controls to the narrator's memory, with the controls themselves parodied to reflect the events and the comic concerns of the narrative. "The rendering style draws from computer games," he says. "The aim is not simply to interest readers to try the book, but also to enrich their reading of it as they progress."

"The tone and text(ure) of the concerns voiced by Western designers would seem comically utopian in India." ITU CHAUDHURI

**TANIA DAS GUPTA**

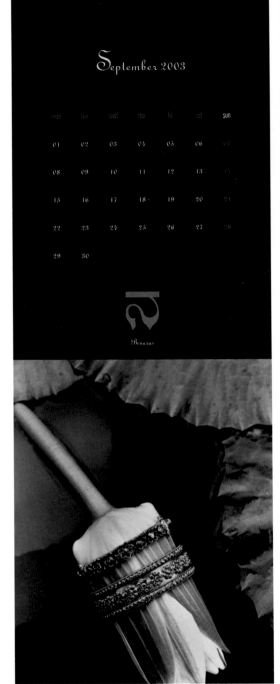

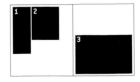

1 Calendar for Ganjam, a traditional jewellery house in southern India, 2003
2 Page from a catalogue for Ganjam, 2003
3 Jacket for *Women*, a collection of photographic portraits and nudes, 1996

TANIA DAS GUPTA STUDIED graphic design at the Government Polytechnic in New Delhi in the 1980s. She gained her first professional experience at the design studio Associated Artists, also in New Delhi, where she developed an interest in typography and worked on company letterheads and corporate identities. She then joined the Ray & Keshavan studio for a short time before turning freelance in 1993.

"I have a particular interest in the evolution of a unique Indian graphics sensibility combining the long tradition of Indian aesthetics with a modern contemporary language," says Das Gupta. While she speaks highly of the work of the Indian graphic designers Dashrath Patel, R.K. Joshi and Sujata Keshavan, she feels that "Indian design is currently a victim of rampant consumerism, and is therefore non-distinctive in the mainstream." Among the Western designers whose work she has admired are the French-Americans Alexey Brodovitch and Fabien Baron, creative directors of *Harper's Bazaar*, New York graphic designer Herb Lubalin, and Fred Woodward, Art Director of *Rolling Stone* magazine.

One of Das Gupta's projects from 2003 was to create a new image for Ganjam, a traditional jewellery house in southern India. Her aim was to design an appropriate image for the international market that still retained its Indian essence. "The challenge was to take upbeat contemporary images and combine them with a graphics language that could be seen as essentially Indian," she explains. "My approach was to take the words Ganjam Nagappa in Kannada script [the company is from Karnataka in southern India] and use that as a bold graphic device in an otherwise contemporary format. The alphabet as graphic device was then extended to catalogues, calendars and diaries and used as a design element in the new boutique. The use of photography reinforced the same approach."

Another project that Das Gupta found challenging and interesting was the design of a picture book entitled *Women*, published by Penguin Books, India, in 1996. "It is a collection of portraits and nudes, a first of its kind in the country," she says. "Because of the sensitive nature of the book, the editing of the images was done by the subjects themselves; they were allowed to determine the appropriate degree of nudity and explicitness. The anonymity requested by some subjects required the images to be cropped in certain ways, and this made the design task even more challenging. The design considerations had to be quiet and subtle so as not to offend any sensibilities in a highly complex and sexually conservative society."

"Indian design is currently a victim of rampant consumerism, and is therefore non-distinctive in the mainstream." TANIA DAS GUPTA

WOMEN

PRABUDDHA DAS GUPTA

WOMEN
PRABUDDHA DAS GUPTA

Introduction by Dom Moraes

VIKING

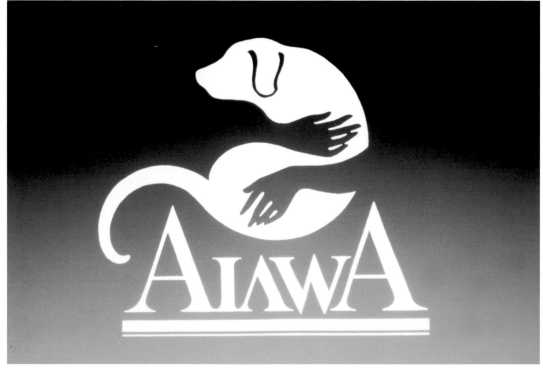

"It has been observed that Indians have the unique ability to live in several centuries at the same time."
SUDARSHAN DHEER

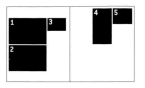

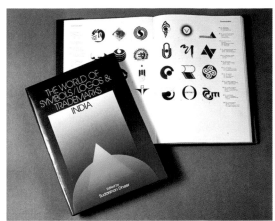

 SUDARSHAN DHEER STUDIED fine art and commercial art at the J.J. School of Arts in Bombay (now Mumbai). In 1974 he established Graphic Communication Concepts, his own design workshop, and specialized in the design of corporate-identity programmes, corporate literature and packaging, and signage systems. He has won numerous local and international design awards, and is included the Hall of Fame of the Communication Arts Guild (CAG).

When he began practising design, Dheer felt that there was not much design awareness in India. Working in the advertising industry, he was exposed to such magazines and periodicals as *Print* from the United States, *Novum* from Germany and *Idea* from Japan, and started to appreciate the seriousness of the design profession. The international designers he most admired were Paul Rand and Louis Dorfsman from the United States, F.H.K. Henrion, Alan Fletcher and Bob Gill from Britain, and Ikko Tanaka, Takenobu Igarashi and Shigeo Fukuda from Japan.

According to Dheer, advertising agencies dominate the visual-communication environment in India. He points out that, since the introduction of an open-door policy by the Indian government some years ago, the economy has been globalized and designers have been faced with a particular challenge. "Unlike any country on this planet, India has inherent cultural aspects that cannot be overlooked by designers," he says. "It has been observed that Indians have the unique ability to live in several centuries at the same time. The Indian designer has little option but to learn how to communicate effectively across fourteen different languages with hundreds of dialects, and across six major religions. The graphic designer has to create order out of this seeming chaos. The designer tries to work from inside out to find the path of the inner self, and to appeal directly to the senses and emotions."

One 1976 project for Dheer was the design of a visual concept for Kissan Food Products. He explains that '*kissan*' is a Hindi word for 'farmer', and is therefore an appropriate brand name for a line of food products that includes jams, sauces, jellies and squashes. "I felt it was important to capture the tongue's experience while eating these products, and the hand's experience while, for example, spreading Kissan jam. So the ripple floating from the K helps to achieve the tactile and tongue experience that is an integral part of the word mark."

"Japanese animation ... developed as an industry and also as culture. ... It moved a still picture, gave life to characters, and expressed the creator's thoughts and beliefs."
TAKASHI AKIYAMA

1   Promotion for Akiyama's posters, 2000
2   Packaging design for a rice product, 2002
3   Cover for the summer issues of *Product Guide*, 2002
4   Symbol for Tama Industries, 1998
5   *What's Justice?*, a poster for Victor JVC, 2001
6   Poster for a conservation event, 1996

TAKASHI AKIYAMA STUDIED graphic design at Tama Art University and Tokyo National University of Fine Arts and Music in the 1970s. He has been awarded an Honorary Doctorate in Philosophy in Art by IOND University (USA), and has won numerous international awards for his posters and other examples of graphic design. His work has been exhibited widely both in Japan and abroad. Some of the influences on Akiyama's approach to design are reflected in the following extracts from his written notes:

"My original scenery: 'Sometimes, when I return to my home town, Nagaoka, I get the sensation of the beauty of nature in the Nagaoka Mountains and the Shinano River: the white snowy scenery and its life; the harvesting time in the autumn gold; the splendid world of the summer fireworks. This is the scenery of a beautiful harmony, and this is my original scenery.'"

"Playing in the poster woods: 'Poster woods are deep. I had been walking around them so long, and I found myself not knowing where I was ... then I woke up. The poster woods had scents. The one I was interested in was filled with a humorous, pleasant scent.'"

"Ukiyo-e: 'This was people's art born in the Edo period, and it has moulded the aesthetic of Japanese designers to the present day. It offered a picture of a transitory world, and demonstrated the most fashionable customs at that very moment. The two main subjects were women and kabuki actors. Among all techniques, the use of the single line is especially attractive. The delicate yet vivid outline reveals the artist's strong will and sensitivity. The simple colour structure and the naïve colour plane remind us of traditional Japanese simplicity. This use of line and colour has deeply influenced my work.'"

"Japanese animation: 'It developed as an industry and also as culture. The first TV animation, called *Atom, The Iron Arm*, was created by Osamu Tezuka in the 1930s. It gave us a hope and a dream, and formed our morals. It moved a still picture, gave life to characters, and expressed the creator's thoughts and beliefs.'"

"*Takashi Akiyama Recycle Notebook* 1999: 'It was common in the 1930s for people to use newspaper flyers as notebooks. People nowadays would think this habit ridiculous, so I decided to revive it. I aimed to reintroduce the symbol of recycling. I may have gone too far, yet it might be valuable as a new form of design.'"

電子・機械技術者のための

# 製品ガイド

## PRODUCTS GUIDE SPECIAL ADVERTISING SUPPLEMENT

**NE** NIKKEI ELECTRONICS 日経エレクトロニクス

**D&M** 日経メカニカル design and manufacturing

日経マイクロデバイス NIKKEI MICRODEVICES

NIKKEI モノ作りのためのIT活用誌 日経デジタル・エンジニアリング **DIGITAL ENGINEERING**

2002 夏号

## 関連展示会カレンダー 一挙掲載!!

2002年6月 ～ 2002年9月

資料請求を
していただくと
プレゼントが当たります!!

**PRESENT**

詳しくは
8ページを!!

インターネット版 製品ガイドも充実!
## http://sg.nikkeibp.co.jp
に今すぐ アクセス

TAMA

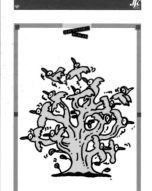

Women of the Century; Suntory Museum

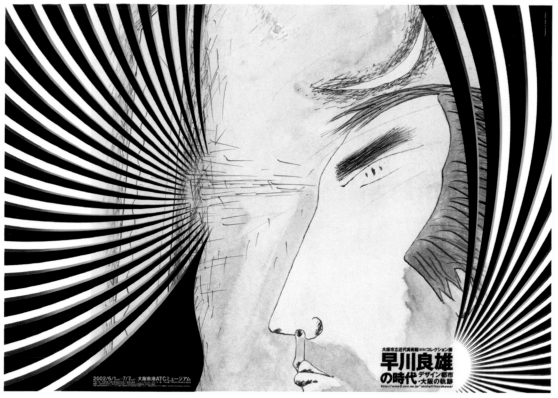

1 Poster for an exhibition entitled *Women of the Century* at the Suntory Museum, 1994
2 Promotional poster for the Japan Graphic Designers Association postcard exhibition *Hana Hana Hana* ('flower'), 1998
3 Promotional poster for an exhibition by Keizo Matsui, 1999
4 Poster for a sixty-year retrospective of the work of the illustrator Yoshio Hayakama, 2002
5 Packaging design for Suntory Whisky, 1989
6 Gift box representing Earth, 1999

KEIZO MATSUI WAS BORN IN Hiroshima, and after studying at the Art University of Osaka he began working in the advertising department of Takashimaya Department Store. In 1984 he established his own studio, which in 1992 became Hundred Design Inc. His design work, for clients throughout the world, includes corporate identity, signage, packaging, poster and exhibition design, and product development.

Matsui has won a number of international design awards, including the Icograda Excellence Award at the 15th International Biennale of Graphic Design, Brno, the Golden Bee Award at the International Biennale of Graphic Design in Moscow and the Gold Prize at the Japan Package Design Awards. He has been selected as a juror for international graphic-design and poster competitions in China, Finland and Russia, and his work has been featured in a number of international design publications.

According to Matsui, the creativity of ancient peoples has been a source of great inspiration to him during his development as a graphic designer. "Their access to external information was limited," he says, "so they intensively expressed their inner worlds. Nowadays, information is widespread and we are constantly bombarded with imagery, and I feel that this inhibits our imagination and creativity. Throughout my career my designs have taken on many forms, but my search for innovation remains unchanged." He espouses the notion of the 'global village', through which cultural interchange has blurred national differences. "I do not search for distinctiveness in countries, but in individuals."

Matsui acknowledges that, for designers, the computer has become "omnipresent and omnipotent". Although he has no intention of fighting its influence, he still considers traditional techniques to be very important, and is continually looking at ways of expressing the merits of traditional approaches through digital technology. A packaging project for Suntory Whisky gave Matsui the opportunity digitally to manipulate photographs of traditional whisky bottles into the shapes of Venus and an angel. "Has there ever been a bottle that can provide the drinker with such a fantasy, and a certain type of narcissism?" he asks. In another project he designed gift boxes representing Earth, with the lid reflecting the cosmos and the inside of the box molten magma.

Where can Nature go?

U.G. SATO STUDIED AT THE Kuwasawa Design School in Tokyo, and after working for a time at the Oka Studio he established Design Farm Inc. in Tokyo in 1975. He is a member of the Alliance Graphique Internationale (AGI) and JAGDA, and among his many international awards have been the Gold Prize at the International Biennale of Graphic Design in Brno (1978) and the Poster Biennale in Lahti (1979), and the Golden Bee Prize at the International Biennale of Graphic Design in Moscow (1998). His current graphic design includes posters, packaging and corporate identity, 3D and animation.

Sato says that he has been greatly influenced by the Ukiyo-e woodcut printing of the Edo period, and in particular by the artists and printmakers Toshusai Sharaku, Katsushika Hokusai and Utagawa Kuniyoshi. The mysterious Sharaku came to prominence when he produced 140 woodblock prints of kabuki actors and sumo wrestlers within a ten-month period in 1794, and then suddenly disappeared. Hokusai (1760–1849) was most famous for his series entitled 'Thirty-Six Views of Mount Fuji', which is said to have influenced Monet and other Impressionists, and Kuniyoshi (c. 1797–1861) for trompe l'œil using figures of men and animals.

"I admired the simple and bold expression of their brushed-line drawing," says Sato. "I was influenced as well by the humour of Raymond Savignac in his vintage posters, the esprit of René Magritte and the illusion of M.C. Escher. In Japan today the trend is towards a combination of aesthetic and technical design. I like the illusory design of the Japanese photo-designer Susumu Endo, who combines traditional offset lithography with modern digital technology."

In 1972, soon after graduating from design school, Sato held a one-man exhibition of silkscreen prints entitled *My Theory of Evolution*, which focused on ecological issues. "This was a very important event in my development as a designer," he says, "because I established how to design by myself using humorous images and illusory vision."

He nominates as one of his most memorable later projects an anti-nuclear poster completed in 1995: "I organized a poster campaign to oppose the French nuclear testing in the Pacific, and, working by fax and in co-operation with the celebrated French graphic designer Gérard Paris-Clavel in Paris, I arranged exhibitions of 150 posters in both Tokyo and Paris. My own poster for the exhibition, entitled *Non Aux Essais Nucléaires*, was awarded the Gold Prize at the International Poster Biennale in Warsaw in 1996."

TSUCHIDA

QUILT KEIKO

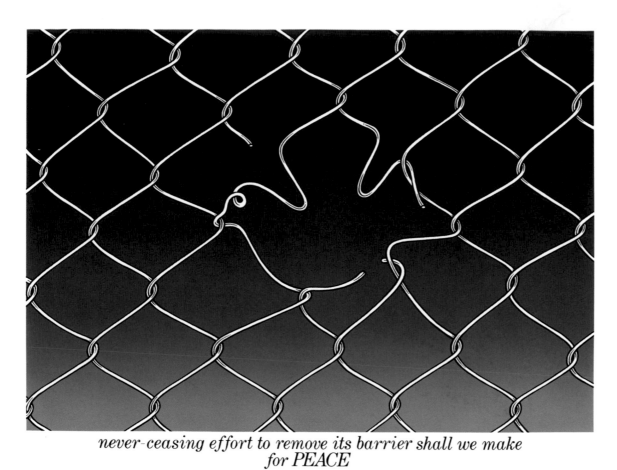

*never-ceasing effort to remove its barrier shall we make*
*for PEACE*

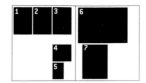

"In Japan today the trend is towards a combination of aesthetic and technical design." U.G. SATO

TADANORI YOKOO

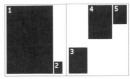

1 Poster on the theme 'Yume no Ukihashi' ('the floating bridge of dreams'), 2001
2 Poster for an exhibition at the Laforet Museum, Harajuku, 2000
3 Poster promoting natural Japanese spas, 2002
4 Poster for a retrospective of Yokoo's work, 2002
5 Poster commemorating the Japanese writer Yukio Mishima, 2000

> "I am now at the point where I create so I can enjoy myself." TADANORI YOKOO

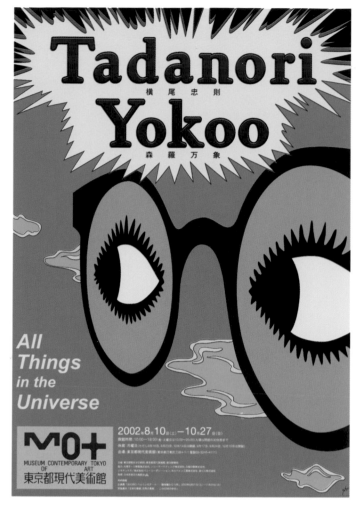

THE WORK OF CELEBRATED designer and painter Tadanori Yokoo spans nearly half a century. A retrospective at the Museum of Contemporary Art in Tokyo, held in 2002 and entitled *All Things in the Universe*, comprised posters, photographs, paintings, sculpture and installations, as well as hundreds of picture postcards of waterfalls. In a review of the exhibition, the critic Monty DiPietro described Yokoo's work as "strident, nationalistic, homoerotic, funny, cosmic, and both representational and abstract". He referred to Yokoo as "somewhat of an international cult figure, and a geyser of creative energy".

Yokoo reveals that as a designer he is self-educated. As a child in the 1950s he showed an early talent for illustration and calligraphy, and won several national competitions. He developed a fascination with manga art and contributed regularly to the magazine *Manga Shonen* (Comic Youth). By the age of twenty-one he was winning competitions for his poster and logo designs as well as for his book and magazine illustrations. He mastered various techniques of graphic reproduction, including black line-drawing and photomontage, and his later period features experimental work with motorized and back-lit constructions that he calls 'technamations'.

Most of Yokoo's poster design was completed during the 1970s and 1980s, before he began focusing on painting and installations. "The main influences on my posters came from Japanese traditions and the Japanese culture," he says. "I'm particularly interested in graphic design from the pre-war period in our country. I also admire the work of international designers, particularly Milton Glaser and Paul Davis because these two have constantly demonstrated that they have human charms as well as design skills." During the 1970s and 1980s Yokoo's work became increasingly unexpected and uninhibited, and drew upon influences from Dada, popular culture, electronic media and the supernatural.

The designer says that he has learned a great deal about art and life from his individual interaction with two prominent Japanese artists. One was Yukio Mishima, the famed writer of the tetralogy *The Sea of Fertility* and numerous books, plays and poems, who committed hara-kiri in 1970 in protest at the decline of traditional Japanese culture. The other was Akira Kurosawa, known as 'the Sensei of Cinema', who arguably had more influence on film-making than any other director in the second half of the twentieth century.

Although Yokoo says "I am now at the point where I create so I can enjoy myself", it seems that this attitude may have always shaped his approach.

KOREAN GRAPHIC DESIGNER and printmaker Dr Kum Nam Baik is Professor of Graphic Design at Sungkyunkwan University in Seoul, and was Chairman of the Design Committee for the Korean component of the 2002 FIFA World Cup. He received his BFA and MFA in Graphic Design at Hong-Ik University in the 1970s, his MFA in Fine Art Education at Kyung Hee University in the 1980s, a further MFA in Advertising and PR at Joongang University in the 1990s, and completed his doctorate in Korean Art History in 2000 at Dongkuk University. He is Chairman of the Korean Industrial Artists Association, a frequent jury member for design competitions, and a member of the Korean Society for Experimentation in Contemporary Design.

More than one hundred and forty exhibitions of posters and prints by Professor Baik have been held in Korea, Japan, Taiwan and numerous other countries, and his serigraphy and pigment prints have been selected for the permanent collections of art and design museums in countries in Asia, South America and Europe. "I have been searching for the characteristics of a Korean visual identity", says Baik, "so that I can apply them to my work. I am trying to identify the differences between the Korean visual identity and those of China and Japan, and the way in which we can use these differences to our advantage. I believe that the visual traditions of Korea are very distinct."

Professor Baik points out that there are many young graphic designers in Korea who are gaining international recognition. "They are using the traditional Korean imagery, but they are modernizing it. I love to share my experiences and knowledge with them. I believe it is important for me and my students to develop an appreciation of Korean cultural traditions, and about twice a month I travel with the students to traditional places of cultural significance in Korea. These trips provide me and the students with the inspiration we need for our work."

Design projects completed by Professor Baik in 2002 include a poster for an exhibition of Korean Buddhist sculpture and a series of posters for the Gahoe Museum, the National Folk Museum of Korea, in Seoul. "The concepts for these and other projects", he says, "always come from the questions 'Where are we from?', 'How did our ancestors live?', 'What did they eat?', 'How did they play?', and 'Where do we go from here?'"

> "I am trying to identify the differences between the Korean visual identity and those of China and Japan, and the way in which we can use these differences to our advantage." KUM NAM BAIK

KUM NAM BAIK

「佛教精神」 한국불교조각전
The Exhibition of Korean Buddhism Sculpture
2003. 4.1~4.30 / 국립중앙박물관
April 1 - April 30, 2003 / National Museum of Korea

「佛教世界」 한국불교조각전
The Exhibition of Korean Buddhism Sculpture
2003. 4.1~4.30 / 국립중앙박물관
April 1 - April 30, 2003 / National Museum of Korea

海印寺聖寶博物館 開館

**Haein-sa Museum Opening**
2002年 7月 5日（佛紀 2546年 7月 5日）

海印寺聖寶博物館

1 Posters for an exhibition of Buddhist
  sculpture at the National Museum of
  Korea, 2002
2 Poster for the opening of the Haein-sa
  Museum in Gyeongsang province, 2002
3 Poster for the opening of the Gahoe
  Museum, in Seoul, 2002
4 Posters from 'The style of Korea' series
  for a printing company, 1995–2002

# OULLIM, THE GREAT HARMONY

## THE EXHIBITION OF KOREAN CONTEMPORARY POSTER

EXHIBITION DATE : 1998. 11.25 (Wednesday) – 12.1 (Tuesday)
EXHIBITION PLACE : KIDP (Korea Institute of Industrial Design)

Icograda 2000 seoul

*Seoul Photo-Triennale I Urbanscape - in & out*

"As a result of Korea's location, our country comes into contact with design from many other countries, but we have not yet been able to blend all these influences with our own culture ..." JAE SIK KWON

JAE SIK KWON STUDIED economics at university in Korea before enrolling in a graphic-design course at the School of Visual Arts in New York. After graduating, he completed a master's degree in Communication at the Pratt Institute, New York. During his studies he developed his current design philosophy, which is based upon verbal–visual communication, and he feels that professors Tony Palladino and Bob Gill were influential in this development. Following his studies abroad, Kwon returned to Korea to practise graphic design, and now has a studio in Seoul.

"As a result of Korea's location," says Kwon, "our country comes into contact with design from many other countries, but we have not yet been able to blend all these influences with our own culture, and develop forms of visual expression that suit the times. Recently there has been some movement in Korea towards an understanding of design as one of the most important cultural values. Among the people exerting particular influence is Professor Byong-Gyu Jung, whose Postmodern design ideology sees the graphic designer as the interpreter of technologically formal problems and solutions." According to Kwon, there are many encouraging signs that Korea is taking design seriously, such as the establishment of the Korean Design Centre and the Korea Institute of Design

Promotion (KIDP). There is as well a growing number of design schools in Korea.

Kwon's current work includes the design of posters, books and visual identities. In 2000 he was commissioned to produce the poster for the Exhibition of Korean Contemporary Posters to coincide with the Icograda Millennium Congress in Seoul. The title of the poster, and the theme for the exhibition and congress, was 'Oullim, The Great Harmony'. "The concept of 'Oullim' comes from the Oriental ideology that in order for one to be in harmony with all the things in the world, one must first be in harmony with oneself," Kwon explains. "Although I liked the theme a lot, for a month and a half all I did was contemplate it. I had not taken the first step towards the design of the poster, and there was less than a week before the submission deadline. But then, one evening while I was walking in a park, I saw a long shadow of myself caused by a street lamp. Right away I began the work for the Oullim poster."

**Seoul Photo-Triennale**

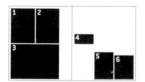

1 Poster for an exhibition of contemporary posters from Korea, 1998
2 Poster for the Seoul Photo-Triennale, 1998
3 Poster for the Friend of Nature society, 2002
4 Logo for the Seoul Photo-Triennale, 1998
5 Poster for the 2002 FIFA World Cup, held in Korea and Japan, 2002
6 Calendar design with Korean art motifs, 2002

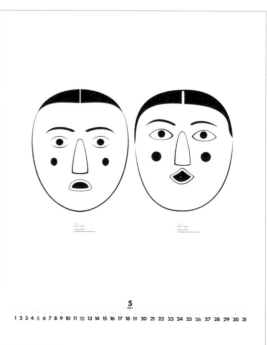

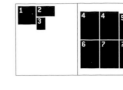

1 Logo for the Social Security Organization, 2000
2 Logo for the Rural Development of the Bolovens Plateau venture, 1996
3 Logo for Lao Telecom, 1996
4 Posters promoting travel in Laos and providing reassurance about AIDS, 1999
5 Poster for General Assurance of Laos, 1999
6 Poster promoting oral hygiene, 1995
7 Magazine advertisements for the Lao Plaza Hotel, 2001

**PRASEUTH BANCHONGPHAKDY**

PRASEUTH BANCHONGPHAKDY was born in Pakse, Laos, and spent his childhood there and in Paris. He studied graphic design and spent some years practising in Sydney, Australia, before returning to his homeland in 1994 and establishing the BlueGrass Design Group in Vientiane, the capital of Laos, in 1996. "The time was right for me to return," says Praseuth. "I was motivated by a desire to do something to help my home country, one of the poorest and most underdeveloped countries in the world."

Banchongphakdy felt that the situation he encountered on his return to Laos demanded a new approach to design. Although the country has a wonderful tradition of art, graphic design is constrained by a sparse population, little industry and few exports. At the same time there are limited opportunities for Laotians to study graphic design, and restrictive, government-enforced regulations regarding signage; for example, private shops are required to use red letters on a yellow background.

"One of the aims of BlueGrass was to use our visual heritage to create new possibilities," says Banchongphakdy. "Laos still has the opportunity to build its own highly distinctive graphics identity, as there is an almost complete absence of visual identity in the country. Public utilities, such as telephone boxes, have no readily recognizable

signage. When I returned to Laos, the only billboards were those devoted to government propaganda." Banchongphakdy believes that the efforts of BlueGrass are having some effect, and that this is demonstrated by the increasing demand for graphics and advertising.

Laos joined Icograda in 1999, and participated in 'Oullim 2000', an international design conference held in Seoul. BlueGrass was selected to be a member of The Design Alliance, a collaborative network of Asian design consultancies from Indonesia, Singapore, Malaysia, Thailand, Laos, Vietnam, China and South Korea; the first annual general meeting of the Alliance was held in Vientiane.

With the keen support of Icograda and The Design Alliance, BlueGrass has been gathering books and magazines from designer friends around the world. These donations have made it possible to establish a small library, called The Design Alliance Library, in the Ecole Nationale des Beaux-Arts, Vientiane. In addition to this, expert designers have volunteered to visit Laos and present the occasional seminar. Such projects also receive the support of commercial enterprises including Arjo Wiggins and Antalis, suppliers and distributors of visual-communication materials. It is Banchongphakdy's profound hope that in the not too distant future Laos will have its own design school.

> "Laos still has the opportunity to build its own highly distinctive graphics identity, as there is an almost complete absence of visual identity in the country."
> PRASEUTH BANCHONGPHAKDY

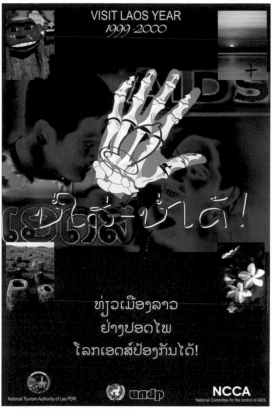

FOC

COD

family          planning

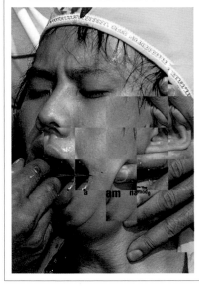

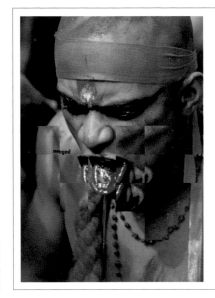

JOSEPH FOO

> "Graphic design began within the advertising agencies in the 1960s, and has been treated as the poor cousin of advertising ever since."
> JOSEPH FOO

JOSEPH FOO IS A PARTNER AT Trinity Visual Communications (3nity) and Trinity Interactive, in Kuala Lumpur. The scope of 3nity's work covers corporate design and includes brand identity, print communication and interactive design. Projects tend to have a strong cultural and spiritual emphasis that comes from Foo's personal approach to his profession.

"I feel that, being both Chinese and Malaysian, I should express Asian thought and identity through my graphic design work," says Foo. "It is very possible that design and the arts can be good for the soul, fulfilling for the designer and beneficial to the audience." This conviction led to the establishment of Art for Soul, a division of 3nity that produces more altruistic work.

After studying design in San Francisco, Joseph Foo worked for a time in the United States and then in Singapore before returning to Malaysia. His growing reputation has led to his involvement as a speaker and panelist for a number of international and local design seminars, and to his appointment as a lecturer on corporate-identity design at The One Academy, just outside Kuala Lumpur.

Foo points out that graphic design in Malaysia is still at a developmental stage: "Graphic design began within the advertising agencies in the 1960s, and has been treated as the poor cousin of advertising ever

since. Only recently have the distinctions between advertising art and graphic design been recognized, and clients are now slowly starting to understand our role. Even so, graphic design in Malaysia is still very much influenced by design from the West, and only a small number of designers are able to see the need to create our own visual identity. The influence of this new awareness is seen mainly in self-initiated projects and pro bono work for theatre and in arts-related projects."

The latest project from the Art for Soul division is 'Man & God', a compilation of thoughts on this subject from designers and artists worldwide. "'Man & God' was inspired by a conversation with my grandma," says Foo. "She asked me why I chose design as a career. What can design do? Can design feed people? Can design save lives and souls? I couldn't answer these questions then, but they provoked me. The answers lie in what we are doing now. Conveying good values through good design is a responsibility we choose to take up."

Taking up this theme, in 2002 3nity initiated *Pahit Manis* ('Bittersweet'), a poster exhibition on "the duality of good and evil", which involved forty designers and was sponsored by the National Art Gallery of Malaysia, in Kuala Lumpur.

"Two booklet of verses – one is for protection, the other of great mercy." Anonymous

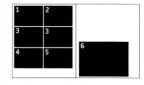

1  Poster from the 'Creation v ManMade' series, 2002
2  Poster promoting family planning, 2002
3  Posters from the 'Transformation' series, documenting man's transformation to god in the context of Hinduism and Taoism, 2002
4  Poster from the 'Creation v ManMade' series, 2002
5  Poster from the 'Man & God' series, 2002
6  Visual documentation from the 'Pocket God' series, 2002

transmission 01

we
love
utopi
a.

JACKSON TAN STARTED THE Phunk Studio in Singapore in 1994 with Melvin Chee, Alvin Tan and William Chan, three fellow-graduates of LaSalle College of the Arts, Singapore.

"We are a collective of information junkies/ creatives," says Jackson Tan. "The influences on our work at Phunk Studio are wide and varied. As we are Singapore Chinese, our background has an influence on the way we think and design. Singapore has a unique culture; it is traditionally a Malay island, but was colonized by the British before the Second World War. Our ancestors were migrants from China. We speak English as a first language, eat Asian food, read American magazines, watch Kung Fu movies from Hong Kong and dig Japanese anime."

Tan describes the work of his studio as "bold and direct, with a unique sense of street-level humour", and he believes that it is radically different from anything produced previously in Singapore. Their work reflects, he feels, a new, extended community of design, art, fashion and music. 'Transmission02:Utopia' is a major project initiated in 2002 that includes a yearly book, an 'e-zine' (electronic magazine), a CD-ROM and a series of limited-edition posters. The project showcases the concepts and thoughts of international contributors working in graphic design, photography, illustration and motion graphics, as well as the written word. The slogan "I Love U(topia)" was used as a design and advertising concept, and it was applied to a book based on the project, packaging, covers, CD-ROMs and associated material.

"'Transmission' is offbeat and a bit cheeky," says Tan. "We were experimenting with a new design format for the site, to break away from the standard way of experiencing an e-zine/web page. You can never do a print magazine with pop-up windows animating in your face ... an online magazine seems the most sensible and natural way to publish the articles we are creating. Web pages were just getting too predictable; we wanted to provoke, entertain and arouse the audience. We've had a variety of feedback about the site; some really hated it and freaked out, while others absolutely loved it. We are still having fun playing around and improving on it."

Another project, from 2002, involved the co-publication of a Singapore style magazine entitled *Trigger*: "For the launch of the magazine we transformed a local club called Zouk into a supermarket, with shelves of products, freezers filled with drinks and staff disguised as shoplifters, security guards and store clerks. It was a lot of fun and an ironic dig at the consumerism promoted by the mass media."

"We speak English as a first language, eat Asian food, read American magazines, and watch Kung Fu movies from Hong Kong and dig Japanese anime."
JACKSON TAN

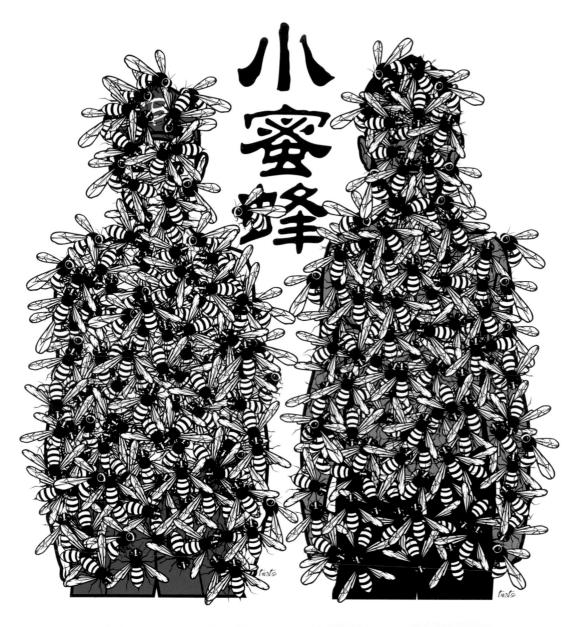

1 Cover of a publication for the 'Transmission02:Utopia' project, 2002

2 Graphic accompaniment to a feature in *Tokion* magazine on the band The Bees, 2002

3 Packaging and visuals for the 'Transmission02:Utopia' project, 2002

4 Poster design and character illustration for a live graffiti event held in France, 2002

5 Graphic accompaniment to a feature in *XLR8R* magazine on the future of streetwear, 2002

現代舞者與書法的對話 (1) The dialog between dancers and calligraphy

SU TSUNG-HSIUNG (JEFFREY SU)

1 The first and second posters from the series 'The dialog between dancers and calligraphy', 2002
2 Poster for the memorial concert of Hongyi, a Buddhist master, 1998
3 Poster for a tour of the United States by the Tsai-Feng Music Troupe, 1998
4 Travel poster promoting the city of Taipei, 2002
5 Logo for EliteGroup Computer Systems, 2002
6 Logo for Auspic Paper Company, 2000
7 Calendar for a paper company, incorporating ancient Chinese sayings, 2000

DISCOVER ASIA. TAIPEI

Designed by Su Tsung Hsiung 蘇宗雄 2002 Printed in Taipei

"There has been a blending of Chinese and Western fashions and styles, and one positive result is the flexible and open-minded way in which designers think and practise."
SU TSUNG-HSIUNG (JEFFREY SU)

# e Herber

 SU TSUNG-HSIUNG, WHO ALSO uses the name Jeffrey Su, studied at art school in Taipei before attending the Graduate School of Visual Design in Tokyo. According to Su, a number of cultural, geographical and political factors have influenced the development of his design philosophy. "Taiwan is a diverse, multicultural society", he says, "as a result of its history of colonization by Holland and Japan, and its proximity to the Chinese mainland. There has been a blending of Chinese and Western fashions and styles, and one positive result is the flexible and open-minded way in which designers think and practise."

Su has an interest in ancient Chinese painting, in particular the art of the Chinese writing brush, and this interest is evident in his work. He has also studied the patterns inherent in the traditional forms of Chinese music, architecture and folk religions, and the links between different branches of the arts. Among his most significant work has been his series of four posters that explore the relationships between dancing and Chinese calligraphy.

The inspiration for the series of posters entitled 'The dialog between dancers and calligraphy' came from the intriguing body language of two young modern dancers and the tension in their movements. Su had been photographing the postures of some modern dancers and saw the possibility of a poster series in which a male and a female, in simple and impromptu costume, danced out the conversation between body and spirit. It seemed natural to Su to combine their postures and gestures with Chinese calligraphy.

"For the first poster", he says, "I chose the four characters Mao-fa Lien-hua from the multiple tower epigraph by Yen Chen-Ching of the Tan dynasty, to show its meaning that 'all great dharma gives birth to the brilliant and holy lotus'. The colour presentation of white background and red characters indicates the peacefulness of the sun at high noon and brightness everywhere.

"For the second poster I chose the character Lu from the seal characters of Lee Yang-Ping. The calligraphy stroke is balanced in its volume, stable but not rigid, and the structure is even and symmetrical, so it looks really elegant. The background is black, with characters in coffee-brown to convey the remoteness of history and tradition, while also conveying the light of mystic civilization." In the other two posters Su drew upon the cursive-style calligraphy of Huang Ting-Chien of the Sung dynasty, and of Taiwanese calligrapher Hsing Tsao from the Ching dynasty.

1 Pages from a passbook for Bank Thai, 1999
2 Packaging for moon cake on the theme of the Year of the Dragon, 2000
3 Poster promoting a logo competition on the theme of elephant conservation, 2002
4 Logo for the film *Hunsa* ('Delight'), 2002
5 Poster for the film *Mon-rak Transistor*, 2002
6 Calendar for the Union Bank of Thailand, 1995

PUNLARP PUNNOTOK graduated with a Bachelor of Industrial Design degree from the King Mongkut Institute of Technology in Bangkok in 1989. After graduation he spent more than three years as a graphic designer with the Samnor company in Bangkok, and then became Director of the Design Department at the Propaganda Design Company. When Propaganda was forced to close, during the economic crisis in South East Asia that began in 1997, Punnotok and his design team founded the Pink Blue Black and Orange Company. This company is now part of The Design Alliance, a collaborative network of graphic designers and artists in Asia.

Punnotok believes that the economic recession in Thailand forced Thai people, including designers, to look closely at themselves and try to find their own identity. "The particular challenge for Thai designers in recent years", he feels, "has been to bridge the gap between the traditions of the past and the economic realities of the present." Many of the influences on Punnotok's design approach come from the traditional Thai world and include Thai alphabets, temples and mural paintings.

One of his most memorable projects has been the design of a poster for a Thai film entitled *Mon-rak Transistor* (*mon-rak* means 'love's charm'), which was shown at the Cannes Film Festival in 2002.

"My objective was to make the poster noticeable among the hundreds of other posters promoting films at the festival," he says. "Also, I wanted to express the main features of the movie, which was considered to be quite exotic, to be fun in a Thai suburban-style way, and to be beautiful. I wanted to pay attention to all the simple little details and to transform them into wonderful design elements. By adopting these approaches, I was able to make the poster quite successful in terms of its design and distinctiveness."

Punnotok's poster for the Chang Foundation of Thailand was designed to publicize a logo contest for the foundation. "'*Chang*' is the Thai word for 'elephant', and the idea of the logo contest was to reinforce the importance of preserving elephants, particularly because the elephant is the traditional symbol of Thailand. The poster was intended to promote a beautiful image of the Thai elephant, and to encourage the contest participants to use interesting typography along with Eastern-style imagery and ideas."

**PUNLARP PUNNOTOK**

"The particular challenge for Thai designers in recent years has been to bridge the gap between the traditions of the past and the economic realities of the present."
PUNLARP PUNNOTOK

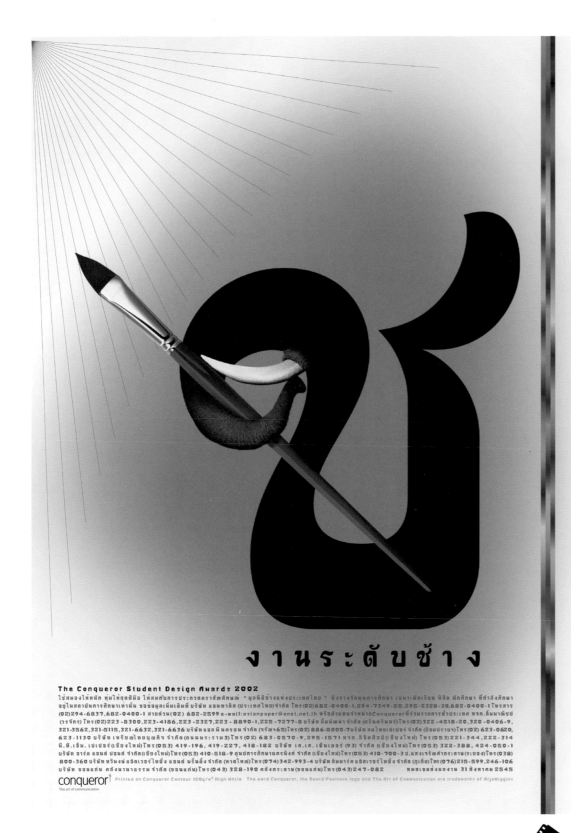

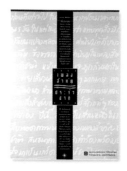

บริษัท ภาพยนตร์ หรรษา จำกัด

EUGENE

The right choice today for a successful tomorrow

**PACIFIC**
ADVERTISING
*THE RIGHT CHOICE*

PACIFIC ADVERTISING & TRADING CO. LTD., 6™ Flr, Me Linh Point Tower, 2 Ngo Duc Ke St., Dist. 1, HCMC, Vietnam. Tel: 848 8299 940/749 Fax: 848 8299974 Email: pacific-ad@hcm.fpt.vn ©2000

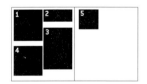

1 Logo for the Studio of Pius Eugene, 2000
2 Logo for a beauty salon in Ho Chi Minh City, 1998
3 Poster based on the Year of the Dragon, 2000
4 Promotion for a Unilever Vietnam event, 2002
5 Label for Bière Larue, which has been brewed in Vietnam since 1909, 1998

PIUS EUGENE WORKS IN HO Chi Minh City as a creative consultant specializing in "design and visual development for advertisements, posters and promotions, cultural events, outdoor advertising, catalogues and brochures, packaging, logos and corporate identities".

Eugene explains that Ho Chi Minh City is his adopted home, as he was born and educated in Malaysia. He graduated in 1982 from the Malaysian Institute of Art, where he had studied graphic design, art and photography. After working for a few years for the international firm Ogilvy & Mather, he established the Studio of Pius Eugene in 1987. He later joined Cato Design before becoming a founding partner of Hamandar Singh's Sledgehammer Communications, publisher of the advertising and communications magazine *ADOI*. In 1996 he arrived in Vietnam to join McCann-Erickson Worldwide. At present, he is an associate of The Design Alliance, a collaborative network of Asian design consultancies.

According to Eugene: "Vietnam has traditionally been the centre for graphic design in Indochina." All currency for the region is designed and printed in Vietnam. Graphic design work used to be concentrated on political posters, stamps, publications and packaging, but the rapidly growing popularity of the photographic, fashion and music industries has created new opportunities. Eugene's Vietnamese clients have included the Asia Dragon Trading Company, Fosters Tien Giang Ltd, O'Brien's Factory, Saigon, Hai Dang Design and the Hoi An Tourist Service Company. "In 1998", he says, "I helped save the 'Tiger' of Danang through my facelift, redesign and graphics for the Tiger beer label Bière Larue."

Eugene finds it strange that, although there are a number of art colleges in Vietnam, there are no courses that focus specifically on graphic design. This situation should change, he says, as creative departments in multinational advertising agencies are moving into Vietnam and encouraging local art directors and writers to develop fresh and original ideas. He points out that the Vietnam office of Saatchi & Saatchi in Ho Chi Minh City was nominated International Agency of the Year in 2001. The positive influence of this advertising agency, he feels, is one of many factors that are prompting more local people to take up graphic design.

Bienvenidos

Mole De
Cadera
$50
Lo Bueno Cuesta

Pase Usted

Bulimia

Diseño: Pablo Kunst / 1er Salón Internacional del Cartel ADA / 98 - Alianza de Diseñadores Argentinos / Tucumán, Argentina 1998

1

THE GRAPHIC DESIGNERS FROM THE Latin American region who are represented in this section are from countries in Central and South America where the modern language is Spanish or Portuguese. Graphic design in Latin American countries has its origins in the visual narratives of pre-Hispanic textiles, tapestries and paintings. The heritage of pre-Hispanic art survives in Mexico and in the north and central Andes, where such peoples as the Aztecs, the Maya and the Incas developed sophisticated civilizations. The visual narratives of these cultures featured representations of mythical figures as well as naturalistic images of animals, plants and humans.

While contemporary graphic designers in the Latin American region occasionally draw upon pre-Hispanic culture in their work, most are increasingly likely to reflect visual influences from more modern times. Colombian designer Professor David Consuegra is one who incorporates the native ornament of Latin America, for example geometrical motifs and anthropomorphic and zoomorphic figures, into the design of corporate identity. Argentinian designer Ricardo Drab invokes contemporary national mythology like the tango and gauchos, and human icons like Evita and Maradona. Others, including Brazilian designer Veronica d'Orey, like to use imagery from their country's natural environment, such as the rain forest and beaches.

Among the most powerful influences on graphic designers of Latin America has been the revolutionary Cuban poster movement that erupted after the overthrow of General Fulgencio Batista by Fidel Castro in 1959. Encouraged by Castro's call to artists and intellectuals to rediscover their creative spirit, graphic designers including Raúl Martínez drew upon indigenous Cuban art to promote the people's struggle. In his book *Posters* (1998), John Barnicoat talks of the combination by Cuban poster designers of the decorative styles of the West with the message of the East. According to Barnicoat, "their posters include frequent quotations from the commercial advertisement and from psychedelic, Pop Art, comic-strip and film posters of the United States' consumer society".

The example of Cuban poster design demonstrates the power of the poster medium to spread social and political messages to large numbers of the population. This power had been demonstrated by the successes of the forerunners of the Cuban poster – the Taller de Gráfica Popular (Workshop for Popular Graphic Art) established in Mexico City in 1937, Polish film and political posters from the 1950s, and the political poster campaigns in Russia and China during their communist eras. Castro's government in Cuba, following the examples set in Russia and China, allocated state resources for artistic and cultural projects, including the design and

production of mass-poster campaigns. The state sponsorship of poster design in Cuba continues today through Editora Política (EP), the official publishing department of the Cuban communist party. Other important non-commercial sponsors of posters are the Cuban Film Institute (ICAIC) and the Organization in Solidarity with the People of Africa, Asia and Latin America (OSPAAAL). The latter is the main producer of international solidarity posters in Cuba and the publisher of *Tricontinental* magazine, which, since 1967, has provided a written and visual commentary on international social and cultural issues.

The poster traditions of Mexico have also contributed greatly to the development of graphic design in the Latin American region. The Taller de Gráfica Popular (TGP) was a co-operative print and poster workshop that aimed to communicate the social, political and economic struggles of the Mexicans that continued after the 1910 revolution. Mexican artists wishing to further the aims of the revolution had already established, in 1933, La Liga de Escritores y Artístas Revolucionarios (The League of Revolutionary Writers and Artists, or LEAR), and they collaborated on posters and murals on revolutionary themes. Among the first projects undertaken by the TGP were the print portfolios *En Nombre de Cristo* (In the Name of Christ) and *La España de Franco* (The Spain of Franco), as well as a number of anti-fascist poster campaigns.

The Mexican poster tradition continues through the International Biennial of the Poster in Mexico, initiated by Professor Xavier Bermúdez and first held in 1990. The seventh biennial, held in Mexico City from October 2002 to January 2003, was aimed at "reinforcing the graphic-design practice in Mexico, as well as acting as an international point of reference and encounter for professionals in the field of design, enhancing awareness and promotion of social subjects that are universally essential". Participants, who include design students as well as leading practitioners, submitted posters for assessment by an international jury in the categories Street Traffic Posters, Small Edition Posters, Computer Design Posters and Unpublished Posters on the theme 'The Rights of Nature'. The biennial attracted 5000 submissions from a wide range of designers across North and South America, Asia, Africa, Australasia and Europe, and 200 prizes were awarded.

Among the factors contributing to the relatively high profile of graphic design in the Latin American region are the work of the professional design associations and the increasing numbers of design publications. Most countries in the region have their own professional graphic-design society, are affiliated with Icograda, and are linked electronically to international design activities. Design magazines are beginning to proliferate, among them *Cyber World Design* and *Proyectodiseño* from Colombia, *Design*

# dreamaholic

5

*Designer* from Brazil, *DX* and *De Diseño* from Mexico, and *Summa+* and *Tipográfica* from Argentina. Common themes in these magazines reflect the close interest taken by Latin American designers in both the traditional area of typography and the new area of design for the Internet.

Professor David Consuegra epitomizes the scholarly approach to typographic design that is becoming evident throughout the Latin American region. Professor Consuegra began practising as a graphic designer in the 1960s, and since that time he has combined design practice with teaching, research and writing on design issues. One of his main objectives is to foster the awareness that design is a visual language. He points out that his design of books for children has demanded a very different graphic approach from his design for posters or corporate identities. When designing his children's books he has undertaken research on editorial design, written his own texts, and developed a new type of illustration that he calls "evocative illustration".

In his role as a design professor Consuegra has organized type workshops that focus on experimentation with type design with a view to understanding the appearance, proportion and structure of letterforms. "The idea of such a workshop is to look forward, to develop new forms and new parameters that may give form

to new alphabets," he says. "This is achieved by cutting letters, applying geometry, reconsidering proportions, working with hybrids *etc.*" Some of Professor Consuegra's best-known work on graphic identity is exemplified in his design of symbols for the Museum of Modern Art of Bogotá (1963) and for a chicken farm (1981). In these he combined abstract elements (triangles, meanders and nose rings) with letters and figures, in order to create a contemporary image that was closely associated with Latin American cultures.

Professor Consuegra is one of many Latin American designers to acknowledge the contribution of the Argentinian designer Rubén Fontana to the development of typography design in the region. Fontana was Professor of Design at the University of Buenos Aires, founded *Tipográfica* magazine in 1987, and developed a programme known as Cátedra Fontana to assist design practitioners and students with their understanding and appreciation of typography. Another whose contribution to the development of graphic design in the region is widely recognized is Gerd Leufert, a Lithuanian who immigrated to Venezuela in the 1950s and, through his professional work and role as Director of the Graphic Arts Program at the School of Visual Arts in Caracas, fostered a new and thoughtful approach to graphic design. His best-known pieces include *Marks*, a fusion of graphic design and writing, and

CUBA DANS LES CAMPS D'ETE DE TURIST ET TRAVAIL

4   Poster and postcard promoting Cuban
    tourism in France: Ñiko (Antonio Pérez
    González), Cuba/Mexico, 1980
5   Logo promoting Alessandra Migani's
    creative services: Alessandra Migani,
    Brazil, 2002
6   Poster for the 1st Ecuadorian Botanical
    Congress: Antonio Mena, Ecuador, 1987
7   Poster for the 7th International Biennial
    of the Poster, held in Mexico City in
    2002: Xavier Bermúdez, Mexico, 2001

*Funeral Songs*, a series of monochrome works that combine graphic design, sculpture and painting.

In 2001 a group of Chilean graphic designers with an interest in typography established tipografia.cl, a web-based association with the objective of developing new Chilean typographies. The founding members of tipografia.cl, Francisco Gálvez, Rodrigo Ramírez, Tono Rojas and Kote Soto, were aiming to promote the study of typography and the design of new typefaces in Chile, since they felt that both had been neglected. Within months of its establishment tipografia.cl had attracted more than seven hundred subscribers from many countries, and a number of new typefaces, including Fundamental, IndoSans and Menu, had been created. Kote Soto explained on the tipografia.cl website in 2002 that Fundamental was the first of the modern Chilean typefaces, and that IndoSans "[represents] the first Chilean typeface family and reinterprets the formal characteristics of traditional Chilean letters in a contemporary and rhythmical form". The network of international typographers created by tipografia.cl has helped to encourage research and discussion on typographical issues throughout the Latin American region.

Many Latin American graphic designers have had some sort of overseas experience, either as undergraduate or postgraduate students in Europe or the United States, or as practitioners in international studios. This has led to an innovative blend of native and international approaches to design. In some countries, for example Cuba and Brazil, there has been an even more stimulating mix of African, European and native cultures. Edward Sullivan, in the book *Brazil Body and Soul* (2001), points out that Brazil has one of the largest African populations in the world, numbering 69 million in 2001. According to Sullivan: "The Afro-Brazilian aesthetic process emerges from the context, thought and emotional experience of a world view based on African matrixes."

Argentina, on the other hand, is inhabited largely by descendants of Europeans. "That is why", according to Argentinian designer Ricardo Drab, "a lot of people say that Argentina is the Latin American Europe, and that the visions and approaches of our designers are not so different from those of Europe." Drab has pointed out that, although Latin American countries may differ in terms of economic prosperity and opportunities for graphic designers, the influence of the Internet has been felt equally in all countries. "The Internet has arrived with information from all over the world," he says. "It has opened the designers' eyes and made them aware of new possibilities and approaches for visual communication. It has also enabled our designers to show their work to the world."

RICARDO DRAB

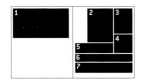

1 Tango typeface, 2000
2 Catalogue cover for *Maxim Software*, 2000
3 Poster from the 'Vans Commandments' series, promoting leisure shoes, 1998
4 Page on Diego Maradona from *Argentina 2000*, a book on the country's icons, 2000
5 Corporate-identity elements for *Olé*, a popular sports magazine, 2002
6 Pages from *Argentina 2000*
7 Corporate graphics for a manual and a promotional project for Yahoo!, 2001

RICARDO DRAB FOUNDED the graphic-design agency RDYA in Buenos Aires in 1996 when he was twenty-one. Prior to this he had studied graphic design and advertising at the University of Palermo (UP), and since the age of seventeen had worked in the creative department of various advertising agencies. Included in these was Agulla & Baccetti, which he says was then the most innovative agency in Argentina. He has also been Art Director of *D/Mode* magazine, and of *Cyberlife*, one of the first technology magazines in the country.

Drab is the Creative Director at RDYA, and the Strategic Director is fellow graphic designer Guillermo Mutis. Together they have created a vision for the studio, which is to operate as both a communication and an art enterprise, combining design, advertising and marketing strategies. In 2001 RDYA published a book entitled *Language*, which reinforces this vision and links it with the studio's approach to visual communication.

According to Drab, while design in Argentina is generally linked to European traditions, it has a number of distinctive features. "The culture in Argentina is different from that of other Latin American countries", he says, "because most of our people are descendants of Europeans. Thus we have European cities, architecture and lifestyles.

However, since the mid-1980s there have been many changes in our country, with the currency devalued by 400% and many companies leaving our market. The challenge for design studios like ours is to do our best at lower cost, to be surprising and cheaper. It is difficult, but possible."

Drab sees many aspects of Argentinian culture and mythology as influencing design approaches and content. These may include elements as diverse as the tango, gauchos, soccer, maté, popular culture and its icons (such as Evita and Carlos Gardel). All these have an impact on the national discourse and help to establish an Argentinian dialect.

The design of the *Maxim Software* magazine is nominated by Drab as one of his most interesting and gratifying projects. Having informed the marketing director of the magazine that in his opinion its design was "a disaster", he was asked to redesign the magazine in four days for the next publishing deadline. "We achieved this," he says, "and the magazine has become a benchmark for editorial design in our country. A lot of designers collect the magazine because they regard it as a model of 'experimental design'. Although we don't like this term, we are pleased that many people in other countries are surprised when they discover that it has been designed by Argentinians."

"The culture in Argentina is different from that of other Latin American countries because most of our people are descendants of Europeans." RICARDO DRAB

CATALOGO.

insumos
accesorios
software

NU_MERO 5

ibook
nueva imac
monitores
impresoras
scanners

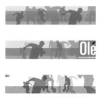

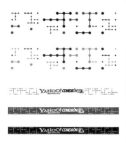

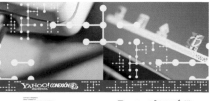

PABLO KUNST

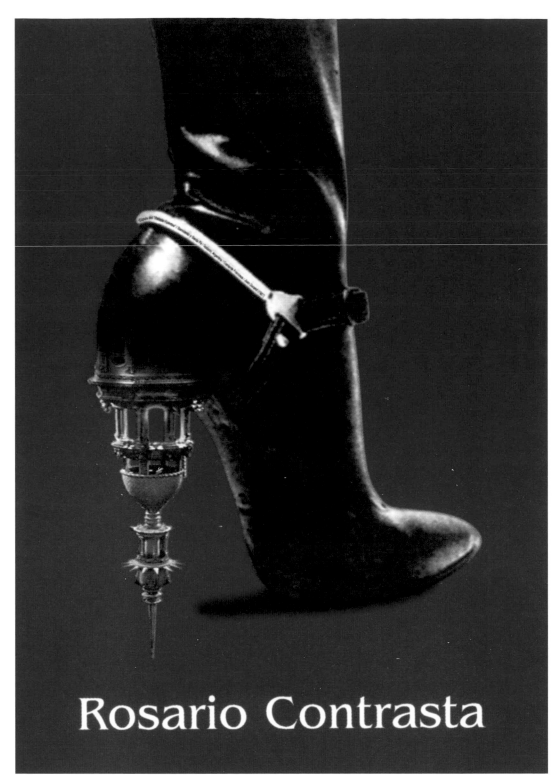

Rosario Contrasta

SINONIMO DE MUERTE

Curso de Educación para la Salud

 PABLO KUNST BEGAN HIS professional life as a creative director in an advertising agency in Rosario, Argentina, and during this period developed an interest in graphic design. "At this time – the 1970s – there was no recognized field of graphic design in Argentina," he explains. "I became interested in the idea of design as a philosophy of life, and realized that the designer has an important social role. Generally, I admire graphic design that demonstrates a strong link to the principles and concepts of design, and is not just concerned with production. A great deal of what we call graphic design should really be called graphic production. Much of it is lacking in the fundamental principles of communication, and brings confusion to a discipline that should be clear and specific."

Prompted by his belief in the importance of design principles, Kunst became co-founder and director of the first School of Graphic Design in Rosario, and he has since been appointed as a professor at other design schools both at home and abroad. He is also the founding president of ADA Argentina – the Argentine Alliance of Designers: "I try to teach design students that it is not good enough to use visual references from Argentinian history, architecture or art, unless they are linked directly with the general principles of design. My library contains design stories, on a wide range of themes, that I have collected over twenty-five years. A process of intellectualization is necessary for the conception and subsequent development of design outcomes."

A significant project undertaken by Pablo Kunst in 2000 was the design of a new corporate identity and other visual imagery for the Municipality of Carcarañá, a city named after the indigenous Indian Carcaraes, known as the Caranchos Devils. The traditional symbol for the municipality was a shield containing an Indian and an arrow, but the municipality wanted to add a number of additional visual elements generated by a school competition. These included the head of a cow and an ear of wheat, to represent farming in the region, a gear lever, symbolizing industry, and some pines, which stand for co-operation between the different local cultures. "The project presented many challenges," said Kunst, "not only graphic but also cultural, as there was at first a lot of resistance from those who did not want the traditional symbol changed. But because of the approach and the thinking that went into the development of the design concept, the objective was achieved and the new identity was well received."

"I became interested in the idea of design as a philosophy of life, and realized that the designer has an important social role." PABLO KUNST

1  Poster promoting an architectural project for the city of Rosario, 1998
2  Poster for the International Biennial of the Poster in Mexico, 1994
3  Poster promoting a course in health education, for the Municipality of Carcarañá, 1999
4  Packaging based on a visual identity for the Municipality of Carcarañá, 2000
5a  Logo for the 4th Annual Book Fair of Rosario, 1995
5b  Logo for the 6th Annual Book Fair of Rosario, 1997
5c  Logo for the Argentine Alliance of Designers (ADA), 1994
5d  Logo for Atlantic Spa, 1997
6  Double-page spreads for a publication of the bestiario (bestiary) engravings of Mele Bruniard, 2000
7  Promotional brochure for Audio Bass, 1999

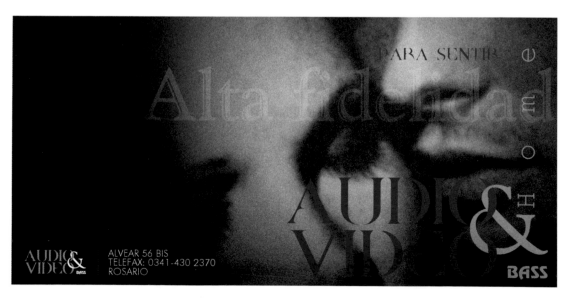

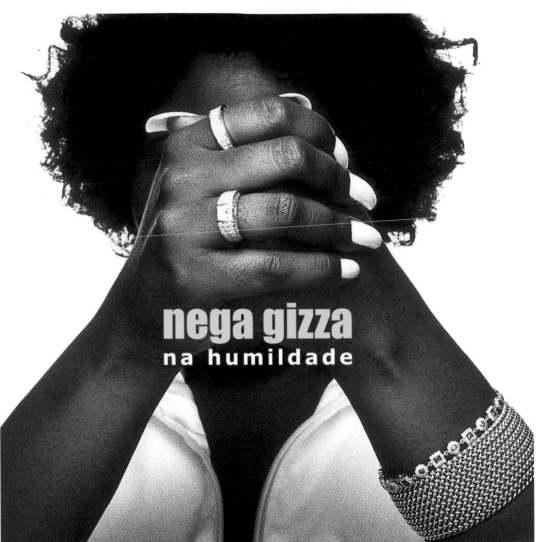

**nega gizza**
na humildade

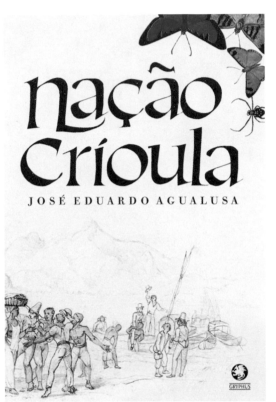

nação Crioula
JOSÉ EDUARDO AGUALUSA

iniciativas produtivas . relações comerciais justas
conservação da biodiversidade

negócios para
**amazônia**
sustentável

PASSAGEIRO

# obi oba

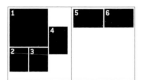

VERONICA D'OREY DESCRIBES herself as a 'self-taught' graphic designer. She studied journalism at university in Brazil, and then worked for three years as an assistant graphic designer for a surfing newspaper. She spent a year at an advertising agency and another as assistant to the designer Jair de Souza.

According to d'Orey, Brazil offers designers a wealth of natural stimuli. "The tropics, the beach, the luxuriant forest and the monkeys by my window push me away from the high-tech, First World trend," she says. "For Brazilian designers there is a mix of popular, Third World influences and vibes from the northern hemisphere. Trying to blend both worlds in a less than ideal situation means that a lot of improvising and creativity goes into making this possible. Gaining recognition for the practice of graphic design in Brazil, and an appreciation of its value, continues to be a heroic undertaking."

D'Orey expresses admiration for a number of Brazilian graphic designers. She singles out Rafic Farah ("surprising, lovely imagery"), Vicente Gil ("good taste, classic"), Nü-des ("young, upcoming, creative"), Marcelo Serpa ("power"), Jair de Souza ("good taste"), Evelyn Grumach ("warrior"), Ana Couto ("business business") and Luciana Justiniani ("great illustrations").

One of d'Orey's most challenging projects was the design of a logo, a catalogue and an exhibition on the theme 'business for a sustainable rainforest'. "I first created the imagery with paper cut-outs and stamps," she explains, "but the client did not approve it, saying they wanted a high-tech feel. I cleaned up the image a bit, but I explained to the client my belief that the force of those products from the rainforest resided in the fact that they were man-made, small-scale productions. So a high-tech feel, coming from an upscale First World factory, was inappropriate. Our aim was to pass on the idea of competitiveness and quality through a careful application of the identity while maintaining the man-made feel."

Another project was the design in 2002 of titles, credits, posters and visual applications for the Brazilian documentary film *Timor Lorosae*. "The images from the film, featuring cemeteries and death, were not interesting or graphic enough as a source for my work," says d'Orey, "so we looked for a cemetery with a desolate, out-of-this-world feeling, and photographed and filmed there. We manipulated it in Photoshop to create the feeling desired, trying to push it towards the desolation and destruction conveyed by the film. The angel, looking up to the sky and praying, also brings a sense of the hope that is present in the documentary."

1 A woman's bag with an ironic twist, constructed from a metric tape-measure, 2002
2 Poster for the Free Jazz Festival, 2001
3 Promotional display for the Free Jazz Festival, 2001
4 Visual identity for a jewellery shop, 2001

ALESSANDRA MIGANI STUDIED at the School of Industrial Design in Rio de Janeiro and then completed an MA in Graphic Design at Central St Martin's College of Art and Design in London in 1997. She has worked as an art director at the advertising agencies ALMAP/BBDO and Young & Rubicam, and is currently an art director at Ogilvy & Mather in Rio.

"My academic background is very much based on graphic/product design and fine art, and my advertising work shows a strong intersection of these skills," says Migani. "My sense of humour and my ability to develop design concepts have come from advertising, my skills at composition and my originality were developed from art, and design has given me a meticulous sense of aesthetics and finishing. While I was completing my MA overseas I was conscious of a very strong Brazilian emphasis in my work, both conceptual and formal."

Migani's design work encompasses posters, books, annuals, cultural events and corporate identities. In September 2002 she launched a private gallery in her house in Ipanema to enable her to exhibit her recent work, which includes approximately one thousand different pieces of underwear, clothing and bags. "I define these pieces as *a permanent exhibition on the body* (the artist speaking), *the body as display* (the designer speaking), and *the body as a medium for advertising* (the art director speaking)," she says. "I avoid the description 'fashion' for the work I do. Although it is supposed to be wearable, I would define it better as 'usual unusual wearable art'."

In 2001 Migani designed the posters and display material for the Free Jazz Project, a promotional campaign for the Free Jazz Festival. The festival has remained the most important jazz music event in Brazil since it first afforded talented young musicians from all over the country the opportunity to perform on a free stage, in 1987. Since the event was sponsored by the cigarette brand Free, Migani used jazz instruments in the design of a pack collection. "Every instrument is at its true scale on the pack, to give a sense of actually touching the instrument or 'playing' the pack," she says. "The communication concept was based on the 'work in progress' idea, from the posters to the scenery of the stage and the whole event. At all times the audience could grasp that such a project is never ready. It is always being built. The scenographers' concept for the stage finally became the display 'Take one' at the point of sale."

"While I was completing my MA overseas I was conscious of a very strong Brazilian emphasis in my work, both conceptual and formal."
ALESSANDRA MIGANI

ALESSANDRA MIGANI

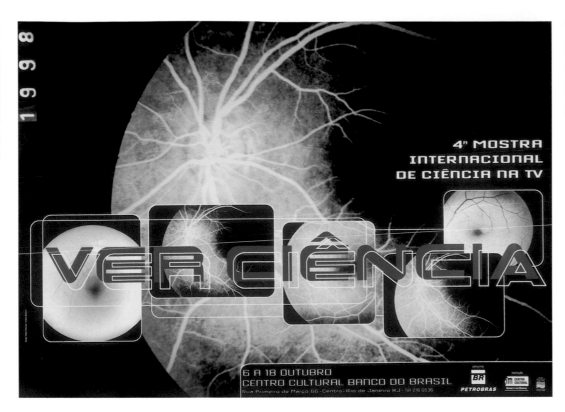

"Comic books and films have also influenced the way I think and design, and they continue to do so. I am still under construction!"

FELIPE TABORDA

**FELIPE TABORDA**

1 Poster for 'Ver Ciência', an international science festival, 1998
2 One of a series of five posters for a dance festival, 2000
3 Poster for a music festival, 2002
4 CD cover for a rock band, 1999
5 Cover for a brochure for the Cannes Film Festival, 1999

WORKING FROM HIS OWN GRAPHIC-DESIGN office in Rio de Janeiro, which opened in 1990, Felipe Taborda focuses on work in the cultural arena, and in the publishing and recording industries. After graduating with a BA in Visual Communication from the Pontifical Catholic University in Rio de Janeiro, he studied cinema and photography at the London International Film School, and graphic design at the School of Visual Arts in New York. He completed an MA in Communication Arts at the New York Institute of Technology.

Many of Taborda's graphic-design projects have cultural themes, and include posters for dance and music festivals, art exhibitions and plays, and covers for film brochures. As well as his client-based work, he has devoted himself to a number of personal cultural projects, such as the co-ordination and editing of *Brazil Designs*, a special issue of the magazine *Print*. Others have included the conceptualization and curatorship of the event '30 Posters on Environment and Development' during Eco 92 in Rio, and of 'The Image of Sound', a project paying tribute to Brazil's leading composers through illustration and typography by contemporary artists.

"My design interests and approach have been influenced by many factors," says Taborda. "We are all products of what we are made of, in terms of cultural influences during our lifetime. Among the many influences on my designs have been the works of other designers, particularly Aloisio Magalhaes, who was the pioneer of design in Brazil. He was such an important figure for many Brazilian designers. Comic books and films have also influenced the way I think and design, and they continue to do so. I am still under construction!"

Taborda and his studio colleagues frequently use personal imagery in their design, and the series of posters entitled 'Ver Ciência' for an international science festival provided an opportunity for this. "Our imagery for this project became a kind of private joke in my studio," he says. "For example, one of the posters featured an eye examination of the mother of Andrea Bezerra, who was my co-designer on this work."

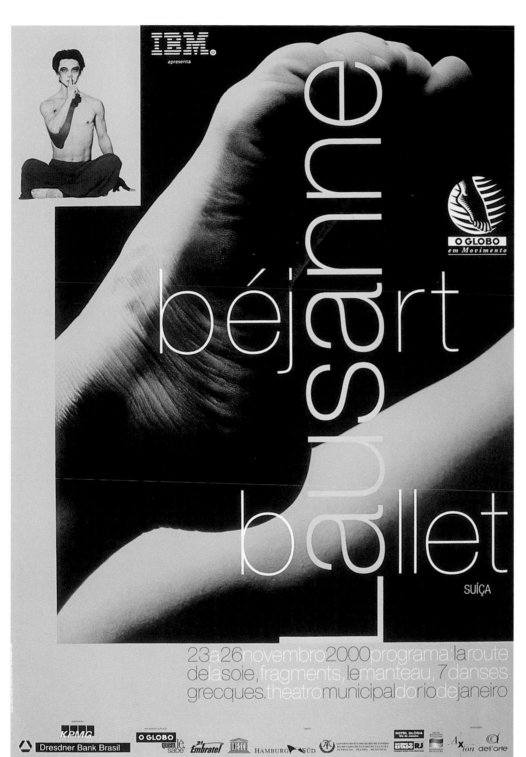

IBM.
apresenta

béjsanrt
lausanne
ballet
SUÍÇA

O GLOBO
em Movimento

23a26novembro2000programa:laroute
delasoie,fragments,lemanteau,7danses
grecques.theatromunicipaldoriodejaneiro

KPMG
Dresdner Bank Brasil
O GLOBO quem lê sabe
Embratel
HAMBURG SÜD
HOTEL GLÓRIA
ESTADO RJ
Axion dell'arte

Banco do Brasil apresenta

Alceu Reis
Andréa Ernest Dias
Antonio Arzolla
Cláudio Cruz
Cristiano Alves
Flavio Augusto
Horacio Schaefer
Igor Sarudiansky
Jairo Diniz
Julio Moretzsohn/Calliope
Leandro Braga
Marcos Paulo
Maria Teresa Madeira
Nahim Marun
Naomi Munakata
Neti Szpilman
Paulo Sérgio Santos
Ricardo Amado
Ricardo Santoro
Rogério Rosa
Silvia Passaroto
Toninho Carrasqueira

MÚSICA
na Semana
de 22

CENTRO CULTURAL
BANCO DO BRASIL

b @ rão vermelho
ao vivo + remixes

GRUPO NOVO DE CINEMA E TV INTERNATIONAL DISTRIBUTION
BRAZILIAN CINEMA

# ÁNIMA
PRINCIPIO DE LA VIDA

EXPOSICIÓN DE PINTURAS Y DIBUJOS

## ADRIANA BENAVENTE B.

DEL 27 DE MAYO AL 20 DE JUNIO DE 1999

ORGANIZA

CENTRO CULTURAL MONTECARMELO

SALA CORDILLERA / BELLAVISTA 0594 (METRO SALVADOR)

MONTECARMELO

Lago Pehoé y Cuernos del Paine, Parque Nacional Torres del Paine, XII Región de Magallanes.

# FEBRERO

copec

| LUNES | MARTES | MIÉRCOLES | JUEVES | VIERNES | SÁBADO | DOMINGO |
|-------|--------|-----------|--------|---------|--------|---------|
| | | | | | 1 | 2 |
| 3 | 4 | 5 | 6 | 7 | 8 | 9 |
| 10 | 11 | 12 | 13 | 14 | 15 | 16 |
| 17 | 18 | 19 | 20 | 21 | 22 | 23 |
| 24 | 25 | 26 | 27 | 28 | | |

**Mobil**

Compañía de Petróleos de Chile S.A.

copec
Primera en servicio

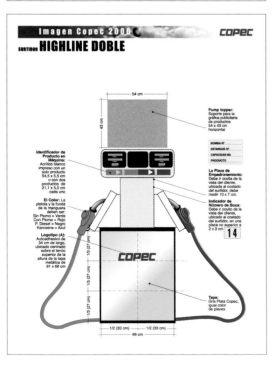

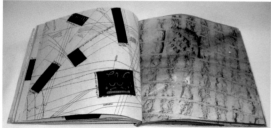

ANDRÉS CORREA ILLANES studied graphic design at the Pontifical Catholic University of Chile, graduating as a Bachelor of Design in 1987. Since graduation he has combined practice in graphic design with teaching at several design schools in Chile, exhibiting his own work, and participating in national design conferences. He calls himself "a corporate graphic designer" and works from his studio in Santiago on company identities and corporate applications. He also undertakes and exhibits more personal work, which he calls "exploration books", employing photography, calligraphy and plastic material to communicate ideas and visual and tactile experiences to "a unique reader".

"In my personal work, such as the exploration books," says Illanes, "I have tried to revive the vernacular graphics of Chile. Among the distinctive features of Chilean graphic design are the use of photography to depict the country's landscape, and the reproduction of traditional Chilean letters in contemporary form, as in the case of the new Chilean typefaces Digna, Fundamental and IndoSans." Illanes has expressed his admiration for the Chilean graphic designers Rodrigo Ramírez, Francisco Gálvez, Tono Rojas and Kote Soto, who designed these and other Chilean typographic families. He admires also the illustration and use of colour of Julián Naranjo and the typographic skills of José Neira.

Illanes's most important corporate clients are currently the Chilean petroleum company Copec and the securities and insurance regulator Superintendencia de Valores y Seguros de Chile (SVS). Other clients include Goodyear, Chevrolet and Itesmap. Since 1998 Illanes has been working on the visual identity for Copec, with a particular focus on the use of the corporate image in company offices and public communication programmes: "During this time I have designed the company calendar in both desktop and mural formats, a corporate manual, and a range of graphic material for evaluating the image of the company's petrol stations and other services. I have been aware of the limited economic resources of the company, and I have tried to design corporate applications that will last several years and will have high market impact while ensuring a high quality of graphic design." Since 2001 Illanes has been developing a new corporate identity for SVS, designing a stationery system, company publications and office signage, as well as furniture and corporate uniforms: "Another agency had designed the logotype, and I had to adapt it to the organization's current needs. The most important thing was to communicate that the organization was an efficient insurance regulator with values that Chileans could be proud of. Again, my challenge was to design excellent graphic systems at minimum cost, and to allow flexibility for design changes in the future."

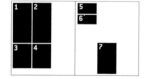

1 Poster for an exhibition of the Chilean painter Adriana Benavente, 1999
2 Calendar for the petroleum company Compañia de Petróleos de Chile (Copec), 2003
3 Folder from a manual of corporate graphics for Copec, 2003
4 Folder from a manual of corporate graphics for the securities and insurance regulator Superintendencia de Valores y Seguros de Chile (SVS), 2002
5 Extract from the book Kitsch by Illanes, comprising visual and tactile sensations based on a L'Oréal catalogue, 2001
6 Extract from the book Restos Mortales (Mortal Rest) comprising personal recollections by Illanes, 2000
7 Part of a personal installation by Illanes held at the Universidad Finis Terrae in Santiago, 2003

"Among the distinctive features of Chilean graphic design are the use of photography to depict the country's landscape, and the reproduction of traditional Chilean letters in contemporary form ..."
ANDRÉS CORREA ILLANES

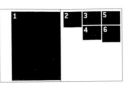

1  Poster promoting Ordóñez's personal
   website, 2002
2  Poster for an environmental event,
   2003
3  Poster/animation on the theme of lost
   boys in Chile, 2002
4  Nuestro.cl, a website developed to
   support Chilean cultural heritage,
   2002
5  *Punto de Luz*, a handmade book of the
   designer's personal thoughts, 2002
6  Cover for a publication on driving
   through Santiago, 2002

CRISTIAN ORDÓÑEZ

http://www.h23.cl

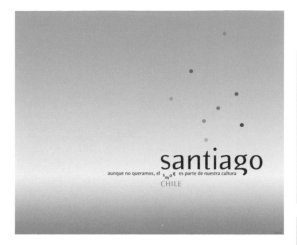

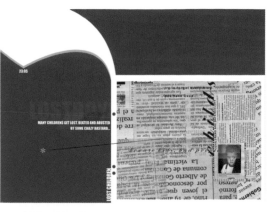

"In Santiago we have acquired a certain lifestyle where we are fast-functioning in anything we create, interpret or develop."

CRISTIAN ORDÓÑEZ

CRISTIAN ORDÓÑEZ STUDIED graphic design at Duoc UC Professional Institute in Santiago in the 1990s, and has since worked as a freelance designer on various projects in print and multimedia. He has developed a personal internet project (www.h23.cl), which he uses to "play with visual elements" and exhibit his own work.

According to Ordóñez, the fast pace of life in Santiago affects the way that graphic designers work. "Santiago has huge traffic jams, and high pollution because of the surrounding mountains," he says. "These factors influence our attitudes, and the way in which we look, perceive and communicate with others. In Santiago we have acquired a certain lifestyle where we are fast-functioning in anything we create, interpret or develop."

Ordóñez observes that, while graphic design in Chile is influenced increasingly by globalization and developing technologies, there are many indigenous designers whose work reflects Chilean traditions: "Some have joined together to form tipografia.cl, a web-based association of Chilean designers with an interest in developing typographies that focus on traditions and typical elements from our culture and environment. Tipografia.cl now has over seven hundred international subscribers."

One of Ordóñez's most significant design projects was the development of nuestro.cl, a website supporting Chilean cultural heritage. The aim of the project, initiated jointly by Corporación del Patrimonio Cultural de Chile and the communication company Entel, was to revive interest in traditional aspects of Chilean culture by providing information and the opportunity for user-interactivity: "Among the images used were those of *huasos*, the skilled horsemen who play a vital part in Chilean parades, fiestas and holidays. We also introduced elements of Chilean houses, with their traditional layouts and colours, heritage locations and Chilean foods. I decided to use innovative ways of interpreting all the ideas, and I was assisted greatly by Rodrigo Ramírez, who created the IndoSans typeface. This typeface allowed me to set a look and a unique feel for both the website and the overall corporate image."

A more personal project for Ordóñez was the compilation and design of a project called *Punto de Luz*: "This is a personal expression interpreting the year that my life changed because of the birth of my daughter, and is a book of shapes, colours and rhythms that reflect the influence of her birth on my life."

DAVID CONSUEGRA IS Professor Emeritus at the National University of Colombia in Bogotá, and has had a distinguished academic career in graphic design at universities both at home and abroad. He completed his BFA at Boston University and his MFA at Yale in the 1960s, and studied with leading designers including Arthur Hoener, Paul Rand, Norman Ives, Bradbury Thompson and Herbert Matter. After returning to Colombia he began a successful design career in which he was able to combine indigenous and international approaches to visual communication.

"My first assignment after returning to Colombia in the mid-1960s was the design of a symbol for the Museum of Modern Art in Bogotá, the first museum of modern art in Colombia. It offered me the perfect opportunity to blend pre-Columbian imagery with an international design vocabulary. It also gave me the chance to structure a particular approach to poster design that marked the beginning of both poster design and graphic design as a discipline in Colombia."

According to Professor Consuegra, there is no such thing as a distinctive Colombian style of graphic design, although there are certain design elements that are characteristic of Latin America's native graphic expression. "Native ornament in Latin America", he says, "is characterized by geometrical motifs (such as meanders, spirals and zigzags), and anthropomorphic or zoomorphic figures (such as monkeys, frogs, birds and people). Because of their geometrical construction and simplified forms, these motifs have been incorporated in the design of corporate identity." Three of Professor Consuegra's best-known symbols, for the Museum of Modern Art in Bogotá, Colombian Handcrafts and the National Television Channel, incorporate these graphic elements.

It is not uncommon for Latin American designers to create symbols for political parties, and in 1985 Consuegra was commissioned to design the graphic identity manual and symbol for the Partido Liberal Colombiano (Colombian Liberal Party). For this he combined calligraphy and geometry to express conditioned freedom, using a wide brush to paint a white 'L' on a red rectangle. It was a powerful graphic statement that permitted him to reconcile graphic expression with the party's political ideas.

Professor Consuegra's graphic work has also covered other fields, which include children's books. He writes and illustrates his own publications, and has won local and international prizes for them. He has also conducted research into graphic design and published a book on American type design.

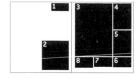

1 Illustration for poetry written by David Consuegra, 1983
2 Symbol for a chicken farm, 1981
3 Poster design for the American–Colombian Centre in Bogotá, 1964
4 Poster for an exhibition of work by the artist Oscar Pantoja, 1964
5 Poster for the opening of the Museum of Modern Art in Bogotá, 1963
6 Symbol for the Museum of Modern Art in Bogotá, 1963
7 Symbol/trademark for Colombian Handcrafts, 1968
8 Symbol for the Colombian Liberal Party, 1985

"Native ornament in Latin America is characterized by geometrical motifs ... and anthropomorphic or zoomorphic figures .... Because of their geometrical construction and simplified forms, these motifs have been incorporated in the design of corporate identity." DAVID CONSUEGRA

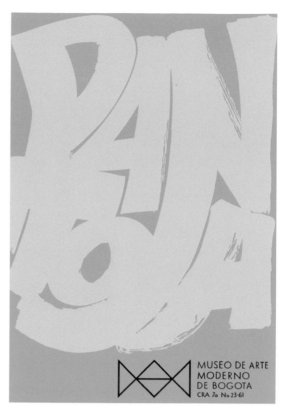

MUSEO DE ARTE
MODERNO
DE BOGOTA
CRA 7a No 23·61

concierto
de jazz MARZO
22·6:30

CENTRO COLOMBO AMERICANO

MUSEO DE ARTE
MODERNO
DE BOGOTA
CRA 7a No 23·61

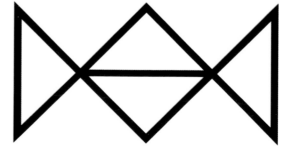

**JOSÉ 'PEPE' MENÉNDEZ**

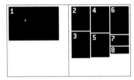

1 Poster for a performance by French circus artists in Havana, 2001
2 Cover for the theatre magazine *Conjunto*, 2002
3 Poster for a festival of French films in Havana, 2000
4 Poster for an exhibition of work by young printmakers, 2001
5 Cover for the art magazine *Dédalo*, 2001
6 Poster promoting the House of the Americas Literature Prize, 2001
7 Logo for a literature colloquium on detective novels, 2001
8 Logo for Cinemania, a Cuban–French film association, 2001

AFTER STUDYING AT THE Design Institute in Havana (ISDI), 'Pepe' Menéndez began practising as a graphic designer in 1990. His main focus has been cultural projects, and he is currently Design Director at the cultural institution House of the Americas (Casa de las Américas).

Menéndez explains that he grew up in a family that had "sensible connections with art". His great-uncle was a pioneer of graphic design in Cuba during the first decades of the twentieth century, and since childhood Menéndez has been surrounded by examples of his work. "My design teachers provided me and other designers of my generation with a perspective on the importance of our profession, the key role that design might (and should, but not always does) play in society, enhancing people's lives. With them we started to learn that design involves much more than beauty, or creativity."

According to Menéndez: "The most distinctive feature of Cuban graphic design is the explosive and incredible convergence of Spain and Africa in one island, visually expressed by a baroque tendency in forms and colours." He points out that Cuba has been an independent country for only a hundred years, and its contemporary visual arts show no strong handicraft or costume tradition, and virtually no traces from pre-Hispanic times. He says also that politics in Cuba has had a big effect on visual expression, and that the country's revolution in the late 1950s and early 1960s inspired new forms of visual communication.

Menéndez's design of a logo for the film association Cinemania in 2001 is, for him, a typical example of how a designer gets inspiration: "I wanted to capture the enthusiasm of the people who collaborate in this association to bring the best of French cinema to a Cuban audience. The name is perfect because it works in both languages. On my way to the office I could see in my mind the similar forms of the letters and the emphasis that I could achieve with both 'i' letters. Additionally, the flags of both nations have the same colours: red, white and blue."

When designing a poster in 2001 for an art exhibition sponsored by House of the Americas, Menéndez was attracted by the idea of producing a link between young artists and young spectators. "Since the artists were young gravure printmakers, I tried to combine this kind of print with the forms of tattoos," he says. "I was looking for a decorative style – baroque and with not much empty space."

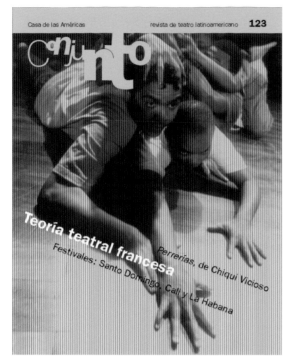

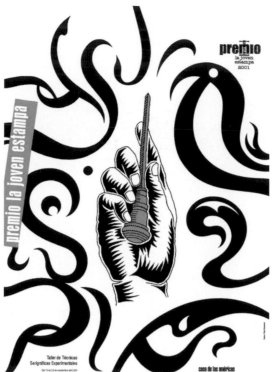

"The most distinctive feature of Cuban graphic design is the explosive and incredible convergence of Spain and Africa in one island, visually expressed by a baroque tendency in forms and colours." JOSÉ 'PEPE' MENÉNDEZ

SANTIAGO PUJOL

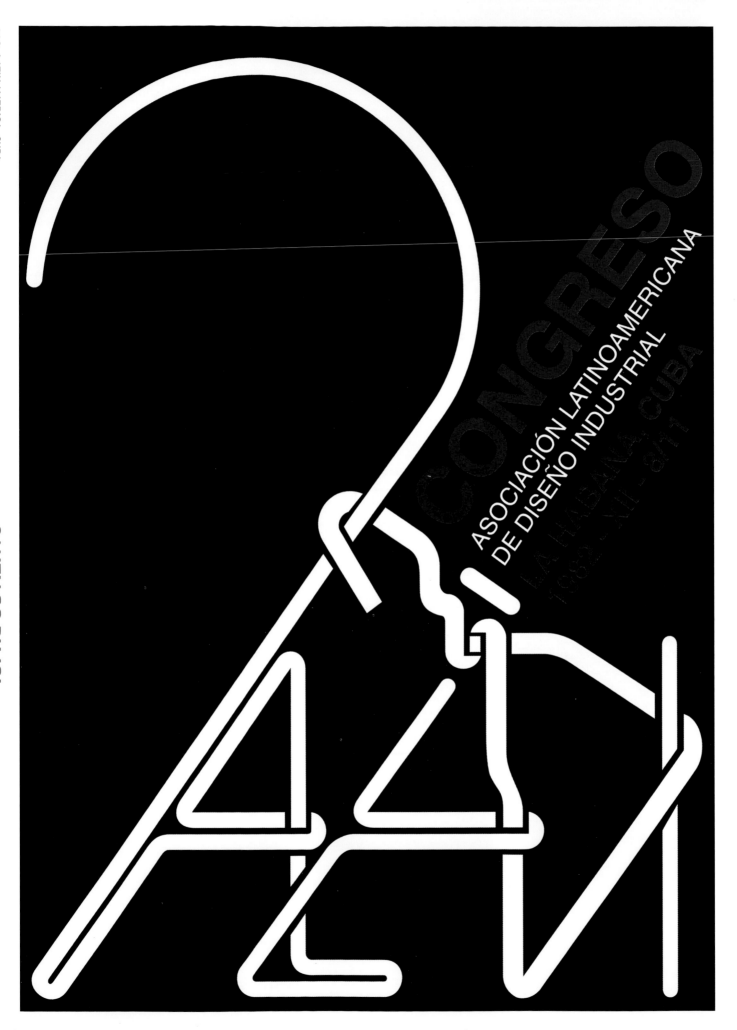

CONGRESO

ASOCIACIÓN LATINOAMERICANA
DE DISEÑO INDUSTRIAL
LA HABANA, CUBA

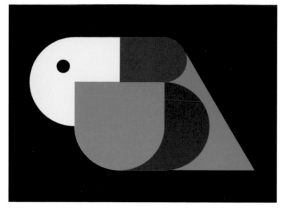

Laboratorios
GAUTIER-Bagó

PRACTIGUÍA
2001

Ética al Servicio de la Salud

"Cuban graphic design has not taken all the force it could have from its own roots. Most clients remain conservative and prefer classic solutions in the European style."
SANTIAGO PUJOL

AS A MUSIC STUDENT AT THE National School of Arts in Havana, Santiago Pujol was introduced to basic design exercises by Professor Felix Beltrán, a noted Cuban designer. He remembers being amazed at the idea of being able to express a feeling or a concept visually within a square inch, or in a poster. At this time, the late 1960s, he was struck also by the power of the cultural and political posters emanating from Cuba and Poland, and he was sufficiently inspired to enrol in Cuba's first university-level course in Information Design at the Higher Institute of Industrial Design in Havana. He considers himself lucky to have "a full audio-visual background", which is particularly useful when he works on multimedia design.

After working in Havana at the Food Industry Packaging Design Center for seven years, and then for eleven years with the National Bureau of Industrial Design, which he helped to establish, Pujol was invited to undertake practical training at Werbeagentur Rechl in Wanfried, Germany, in the 1990s. This experience proved valuable, and since then he has been able to maintain a career as a freelance graphic designer working on both local and international projects. This combination reflects, he feels, the Cuban approach to graphic design. "Since Cuban culture has been nurtured by African and European streams," he says, "the result of their

fusion is a rich and bold, colourful imagery in a quite naïve style. These features are present mostly in popular art and in handicrafts, but I consider that Cuban graphic design has not taken all the force it could have from its own roots. Most clients remain conservative and prefer classic solutions in the European style."

One of Pujol's clients is Gautier-Bagó, a Uruguayan/Argentinian medical-research enterprise, and he has regularly won awards for the company's promotion design at the annual International Medical Fair in Havana. For the 2001 fair Pujol produced a very simple design: a gigantic texture airbrush-painted on a big PVC sheet all around the display booth, which was reproduced as the background for the cover of the catalogue, a calendar and other products. "The idea", he says, "was to convey both the micro- and the macro-universal sense of scientific research with a low-level reference to Kubrick's *2001: A Space Odyssey*."

Pujol considers that there are some young designers in Cuba who are showing the sort of flair that once brought the Cuban poster international acclaim. From among these he mentions José 'Pepe' Menéndez, Luis Alonso and Paris Volta. "They have a special sense of rhythm and colour as well as a strong facility for synthesis," he explains, "and I think that the future for graphic design in Cuba is starting to look good."

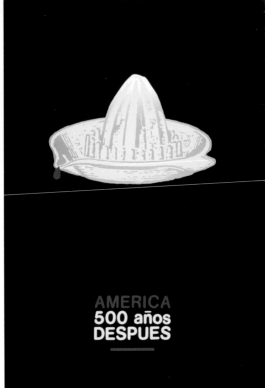

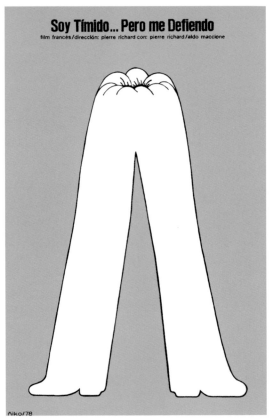

ÑIKO (ANTONIO PÉREZ GONZÁLEZ)

Para Subir al Cielo...

RESTAURANTE
La Sopa

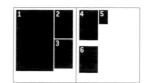

> "I felt that Mexico, at that time, offered me better opportunities to confront and experiment with graphic design, and enabled me to forge stronger links with the international design community."
>
> ÑIKO (ANTONIO PÉREZ GONZÁLEZ)

GALA DE OPERA

PROFESSOR ANTONIO PÉREZ González, known widely as Ñiko, studied art history at the University of Havana in the 1960s, and calls himself a "self-educated graphic designer". After graduating he found himself teaching the basics of design and graphics, and soon began practising as a professional designer. After nearly twenty years of practice in Cuba he felt that his professional opportunities were dwindling, and in 1988 he decided to set up practice in Mexico. "I felt that Mexico, at that time, offered me better opportunities to confront and experiment with graphic design," he says, "and enabled me to forge stronger links with the international design community."

Ñiko is Professor in both the School of Graphic Design at the Benemérita Autonomous University of Puebla and the Gestalt School of Design in Xalapa, Veracruz. He has held professorships at a number of other universities in Cuba and Mexico, and, as a prominent designer, has been invited to Paris, Montreal, Valencia, Warsaw and Moscow. He has written extensively on poster design for books, magazines and catalogues, and has delivered many lectures internationally on graphic design and related themes.

During his time in Cuba, Ñiko won numerous awards and distinctions, particularly for his film posters. Many of these have been for international film festivals held in Cuba and further afield, in Spain, Poland, France, Czechoslovakia and the United States. Since moving to Mexico he has developed his international profile and has held a number of exhibitions and retrospectives of his work.

One of Ñiko's largest and most difficult design projects was for the poster exhibition *100 Years of Movies*, which was held in Mexico in 1995 and featured the film posters of eighteen Cuban and Mexican designers. Ñiko designed the thematic poster and catalogue for the exhibition, and had the task of co-ordinating the contributions from the designers represented. A similar project, entitled 'America 500 Years Later', for the 1992 Poster Biennale in Mexico featured the work of forty-four international graphic designers, and Ñiko once again designed the catalogue and the thematic poster.

"We have more than fourteen ethnic groups, each with its own culture and language, and four completely different geographical zones – the Andes, Amazonia, the Galapagos and the Pacific Coast ... It would be stupid of us to ignore such an incredible source of visual inspiration." JUAN LORENZO BARRAGÁN

## JUAN LORENZO BARRAGÁN

JUAN LORENZO BARRAGÁN established Azuca Ingenio Gráfico, the first graphic-design studio in Ecuador, in 1986. While running the studio, he has also, for fourteen years, been Art Director of *Mundo Diners*, a monthly magazine published by the Diners Club that features articles on architecture, design and other cultural issues. From 1994 to 2000 he was also Art Director of another monthly, *Gestión*, focusing on business, political and social issues.

Barragán studied architecture for two years at the Central University of Ecuador, Quito, before completing a BA in Communication Design at the Pratt Institute in New York in 1985. On returning to Ecuador he found there was no recognized profession of graphic design in the country, and no specialized graphic-design studio. According to Barragán, the best-known graphic designer in Ecuador at the time was Peter Mussfeldt, a Berlin-born artist and designer who had immigrated to Guayaquil in Ecuador in 1962 as art director at a new advertising agency, later to become Norlop-Thompson. Barragán acknowledges Mussfeldt's strong early influence on him, especially his skill in combining fine art and commercial design.

Although Barragán argues that it is impossible for designers from Ecuador to ignore international design trends, he says that he and other designers draw upon the visual resources of the country for their approach to form, colour and pattern: "We have archaeological sites that are more than six thousand years old, with incredible aesthetic associations. We have more than fourteen ethnic groups, each with its own culture and language, and four completely different geographical zones – the Andes, Amazonia, the Galapagos and the Pacific Coast – all in an area smaller than New Zealand. It would be stupid of us to ignore such an incredible source of visual inspiration."

Barragán is a supporter of the anti-globalization movement gaining momentum in Latin America: "My approach to design is influenced by my strong anti-consumerism feelings and by environmental issues. In our studio we try to avoid advertising and transnational corporate clients. We specialize in cultural and social projects, and do pro-bono work on environmental issues. When we develop corporate images for our clients we try to be as honest and transparent as possible." In 1993 he founded the graphic-design periodical *Papagayo*, to which he contributes a column called 'Loreando' (parrot talk): "I criticize excessive spending by local governments on their own corporate image, while I praise original and good work by local designers and artists. The periodical has provided an ideal way of transmitting the thoughts of members of our country's design organization, the Asociación de Diseñadores Gráficos (ADG)."

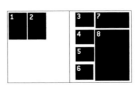

1 Poster for a concert in Quito by the Afro-Cuban jazz group Irakere, 1994
2 Poster for a concert in Quito by the singer and illustrator Hugo Idrovo, 1997
3 Logo for the Latin American Development Corporation (CLD), 2004
4 Logo for Albonova, a pharmaceutical and cosmetics company, 1995
5 Logo for Conteiner, a contemporary art gallery in Quito, 2002
6 Logo for El Galpón, a restaurant and museum in Quito, 2004
7 Logo for Green Consulting, consultants for environmental and ecological tourism, 2000
8 Poster for Ecuador's Bienal de Diseño, 2000

CLD

green
consulting

Albonova

el
CON
TEI
NER

EL GALPON
MUSEO · RESTAURANT

"Our pre-Hispanic cultures dazzle with their imagination and the purity of their designs."

SANDRO GIORGI

SILVIO & SANDRO GIORGI

 SILVIO GIORGI AND HIS brother Sandro established the design agency GIOTTO in Quito, Ecuador, in 1994. Originally from Colombia, they moved to Ecuador in the mid-1980s. They completed their design studies in Ecuador and the United States, with Silvio majoring in Graphic Design and Sandro in Industrial Design. Both feel that their real education has come from the many experiences associated with their identity as Latin Americans. The brothers have worked together on a wide range of corporate graphics projects, including brochures and logos.

Sandro points out that Ecuador, like the rest of Latin America, is constantly bombarded with information from the industrialized nations. "It is almost impossible to turn one's back on this avalanche of information," he says. "Despite this, the country has managed to create an identity that is both endemic and authentic. Our region of Latin America possesses a history as old as that of Europe, but with a heritage rich in distinctive shapes, colours and unique and mysterious symbols. Our pre-Hispanic cultures dazzle with their imagination and the purity of their designs; they represent a group without religious or political influence, and display a marvellous and perpetual authenticity."

Indigenous graphic design in Ecuador, according to the brothers, reflects the picturesque nature of the country. "The colours are pure and intense," says Silvio. "Blue, red and yellow are the essence that enables symbols to penetrate visually and silently deliver their message." The stated mission of the GIOTTO studio is "to utilize the distinctive characteristics of the country and region to create images that communicate strongly, bringing together corporate objectives and the manifestation of lifestyles".

In 2001 Silvio Giorgi worked with another graphic designer, Belén Mena, on the design of a series of posters for a public-space exposition on the theme 'reflections on society'. The posters were displayed on thirty-five street corners in Quito over a three-week period. "Our objective was to create a number of concepts providing a critique on society, each of which reflected a single message, instantly and powerfully," says Silvio. "We wanted to communicate what people really identify with in a country with lots of contrasts and taboos. There were many days of conceptualizing and sketching within bars, discotheques and offices, in both city and country locations. Our ideas were visualized in the series of posters on the themes of woman, man, marriage, sex, beauty, democracy, politics, religion and BlaBlaBla. Concepts that tried to be a shout from the wall; strong reflections that also let us laugh at ourselves."

sociedad:política/society:politics

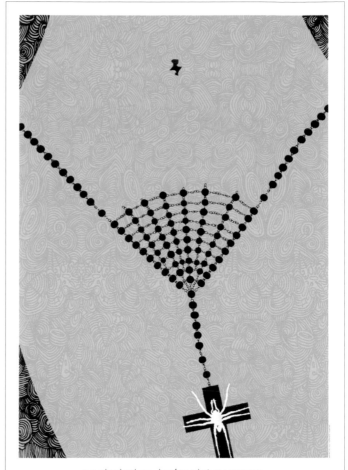

sociedad:mujer/society:woman

sociedad:hombre/society:man

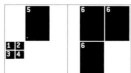

1 Logo for an Internet art gallery, 2001
2 Logo for Enigma Business Solutions, 2001
3 Logo for a group of Quito artisans, 2001
4 Logo for a restaurant group in Quito, 2001
5 Poster for an adventure challenge event, 2002
6 Posters for the series 'Reflections on Society', 2001

SEMINARIO
TRABAJOS FORZOSOS O

¿NUEVAS DE
FORMAS DE
ESCLAVISMO?

7 - 8 de octubre de 2002 • Auditorio FLACSO
FLACSO sede Ecuador • Páez N19-26 y Av. Patria • Teléfonos 2232-029 / 030 / 031 • Fax: 2566-139
frivera@flacso.org.ec • flacso@flacso.org.ec • www.flacso.org.ec • Quito - Ecuador

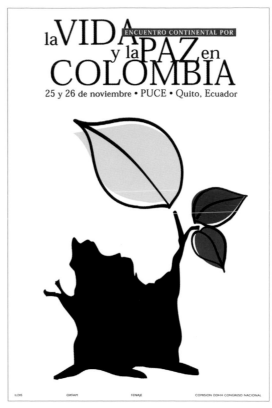

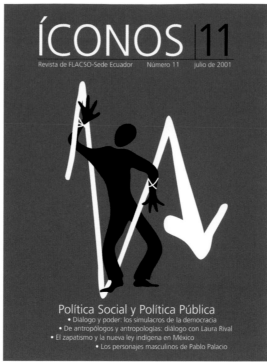

**ÍCONOS | 11**

Revista de FLACSO-Sede Ecuador · Número 11 · julio de 2001

**Política Social y Política Pública**
- Diálogo y poder: los simulacros de la democracia
- De antropólogos y antropologías: diálogo con Laura Rival
- El zapatismo y la nueva ley indígena en México
- Los personajes masculinos de Pablo Palacio

equidad

"I believe that well-understood visual communication can be a very powerful tool in promoting change."
ANTONIO MENA

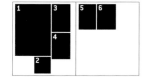

1  Poster opposing 'new forms of slavery', for the Latin American Faculty of Social Sciences (FLACSO), 2002
2  CD cover for a classical guitarist, 2001
3  Poster for a symposium in Quito on the Colombian conflict, 1999
4  Poster opposing 'imprisonment without sentencing', for the Corporation of Latin-American Development, 1994
5  Digital impression on 'The Rights of Nature', 2002
6  Cover for *ICONOS* magazine, 2001

ANTONIO MENA STUDIED fine art for two years at the Central University in Quito in 1980 because there was no degree course in graphic design in Ecuador at that time. He then studied graphic design in Germany at the Kunstschule Alsterdamm in Hamburg. He now has his own graphic-design studio in Quito and lectures at the School of Architecture and Graphic Design at the Pontifical Catholic University.

Mena believes that his work reflects two influences: the expressive force of the chromatic contrasts found in the Andean culture, and the structure and synthesis of German design acquired during his studies in Germany. "Ecuador is a country very rich in visual expression, which ranges from handicrafts to Andean folklore and painting," he says. "Like many other Latin American countries, Ecuador is marked by the diversity of its regions, cultures and socio-economic groups. While it is a country rich in natural resources and cultural expressions, paradoxically a large proportion of its population is poor and illiterate. I believe that graphic design, which is fairly new in Ecuador, has to take into account these realities and, from its particular perspective, work together with people and institutions that seek the development of the country at every level. I believe that well-understood visual communication can be a very powerful tool in promoting change."

A project that held special significance for Mena was his design in 1999 of a poster for a symposium in Quito on the Colombian conflict. This was a virtual war between the Colombian state, drug cartels and paramilitary groups, and represented a threat to the security and stability not only of Colombia but also of its neighbour Ecuador. When designing the poster, Mena felt that his challenge was to obtain an aesthetically pleasing image about an issue that implies death and destruction, and also to extend a hope for peace. He decided to use the metaphor of a tree that is apparently dead and scorched, but from which bright leaves are sprouting.

"I wanted to represent the strength of a culture and a people that refuse to succumb and are reborn with renewed energy, in spite of the surrounding cruelty and destruction. The vital primary colours of the leaves are also the colours of the Ecuadorean and Colombian flags. The public like the poster very much, I believe, because of the simplicity and clarity of the message."

IN 1990 XAVIER BERMÚDEZ founded the International Biennial of the Poster in Mexico, an event that he continues to organize alongside running his own graphic-design studio, Matatena Visual, in Mexico City. After studying graphic design at the Metropolitan Independent University (UAM) in Mexico City he undertook further study at the Polytechnic School of Design in Milan, where his teachers included the Swiss designer Max Huber and Italian designers Bruno Munari and Walter Ballmer. He also studied music at the Giuseppe Verdi Conservatory.

Professor Bermúdez has held the post of Professor of Graphic Design at universities in Mexico, Argentina, Spain and Canada. His career highlights have included the establishment of his first design studio, Troje Taller, in 1977, and of the organizing body for the biennial, Trama Visual, in 1989. He founded the magazines *Via Libre* and *Lúdica* in 1987 and 1997 respectively. His work has appeared in numerous international magazines and publications, and he has been a jury member for several international design competitions.

"For me, design is a continuous and fundamental tool for human cohabitation," says Professor Bermúdez. "It organizes, facilitates, orientates, optimizes and educates. Graphic design is neither fashion nor style. It consists of concepts and the application of our own language in a graphic form. I am not reliant on the new technologies, but rather I look for new design applications. So there is no difference in the basic principles for designing a biennale, an exhibition or a logotype.

"Nowadays," he continues, "new generations of graphic designers mistakenly believe they are creating something new, but I believe that graphic design is the second oldest practice after procreation. We need to open a healthy discussion about the future of our practice, helping the younger designers to learn what is design and what is not design. We should be worrying much more about retaining good design principles."

Professor Bermúdez aims to promote this philosophy in his direction of the International Biennial of the Poster in Mexico. His objective for the festival is "to consolidate a true graphic-design university by inviting great masters to share their knowledge with the new generation of designers". The seventh biennial invited participants to meditate on the future of the relationship between people and their environment. In conjunction with the United Nations, it selected fifty previously unpublished works to form a poster collection for international exhibition from 2003 under the title 'The Rights of Nature'.

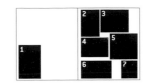

1  Packaging and identity for Murrieta coffee, 1998
2  Poster for the 27th Metropolitan Book Fair, Mexico City, 1998
3  Catalogue covers for the Metropolitan Gallery in Mexico City, 2002
4  Programme covers for the 7th and 5th International Biennial of the Poster, held in Mexico City in 2002 and 1998, 2001 and 1997
5  Covers for *Tiempo*, the magazine of the Metropolitan Independent University in Mexico City, 1999–2001
6  Logo for Trama Visual, the organizing body for the International Biennial of the Poster, 1988
7  Logo for Xavier Bermúdez's studio, 2000

"For me, design is a continuous and fundamental tool for human cohabitation. It organizes, facilitates, orientates, optimizes and educates."  XAVIER BERMÚDEZ

# XXVII
## F E R I A
### METROPOLITANA DEL
# LIBRO

J U A N
GILBERTO
ACEVES
NAVARRO
FELGUÉREZ
SORIANO

Del 22 al 31 de mayo, de 11 a 20 hrs. en EXHIBIMEX
Av. Cuauhtémoc esq. Antonio M. Anza (Metro Centro Médico), Colonia Roma, México, D.F.

CANIEM

**ENTRADA LIBRE**

7ªBICM
SÉPTIMA BIENAL INTERNACIONAL DEL CARTEL EN MÉXICO
SIÓDME MIEDZYNARODOWE BIENNALE PLAKATU MEKSYKU
SEVENTH INTERNATIONAL BIENNIAL OF THE POSTER IN MEXICO

PROGRAMA DE ACTIVIDADES

Edición in memoriam Günther Schmidt, Eduardo Muñoz Bachs,
Marcello Minale, Jan Lenica e Ikko Tanaka

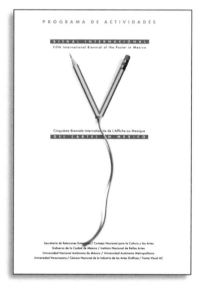

PROGRAMA DE ACTIVIDADES

BIENAL INTERNACIONAL
Fifth International Biennial of the Poster in Mexico

Cinquième Biennale Internationale de L'Affiche au Mexique
DEL CARTEL EN MÉXICO

Secretaría de Relaciones Exteriores / Consejo Nacional para la Cultura y las Artes
Gobierno de la Ciudad de México / Instituto Nacional de Bellas Artes
Universidad Nacional Autónoma de México / Universidad Autónoma Metropolitana
Universidad Veracruzana / Cámara Nacional de la Industria de las Artes Gráficas / Trama Visual AC

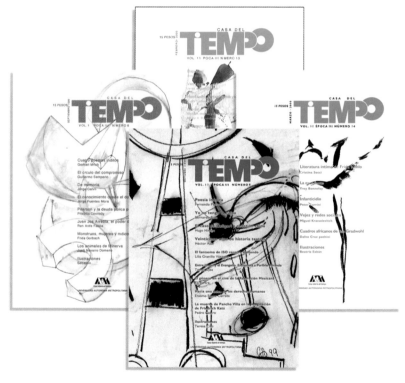

# TRAMA VISUAL

# MATATENA
## V I S U A L

FELIPE COVARRUBIAS

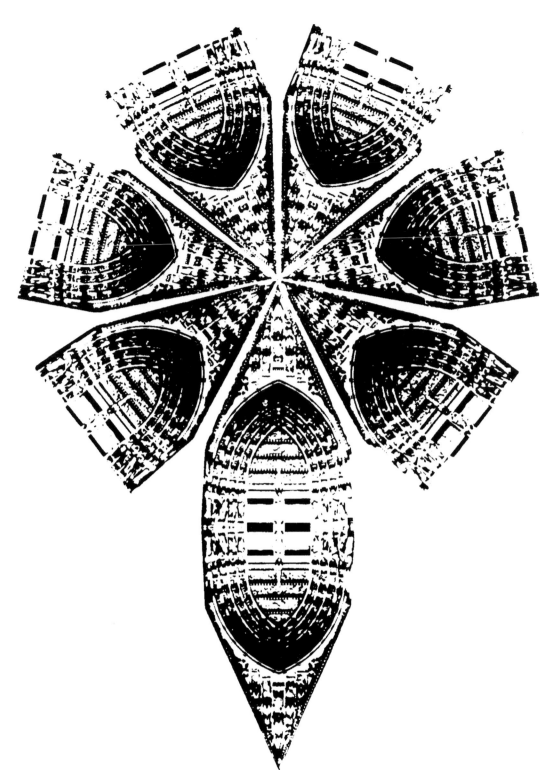

"With regard to contemporary Mexican graphic design, I admire the definitive way in which Vicente Rojo applies design to the cultural environment." FELIPE COVARRUBIAS

AFTER COMPLETING A DEGREE in Architecture in 1969 at the ITESO University in Guadalajara, Felipe Covarrubias began working as a graphic designer in the government's Department of the Arts. He later studied typography and photography in London before establishing his own graphic-design studio, GaleríAzul, in Guadalajara and launching *Magenta* magazine. Since 1998 he has been Director of the School of Design at ITESO University, and has continued to practise on a freelance basis. His work in graphic design and photography has been exhibited widely in Mexico, and internationally, since the 1970s.

According to Covarrubias, the development of graphic design in Mexico has been influenced significantly by Julio Ruelas and José Guadalupe Posada, illustrators and printmakers in Mexico in the late nineteenth and early twentieth centuries. Ruelas, sometimes described as a "dark character", explored through his use of fantasy and mystery the social fabric of Mexico. Guadalupe Posada was arguably Mexico's most popular graphic artist at the beginning of the twentieth century, owing to his illustrations for cheap street-publications that focused on crimes, disasters, religious issues and local heroes. Among the important visual influences in Mexico today, says Covarrubias, are the images on the cards used for such popular Mexican games as Loteria.

"With regard to contemporary Mexican graphic design, I admire the definitive way in which Vicente Rojo applies design to the cultural environment. I am also an admirer of Germán Montalvo because of his refreshing approach and the way in which he revives popular traditions and gives them an international context, and of Rafael Lopez Castro, who for the past thirty years has been addressing the problem of national identity with precision and the utmost quality."

In designing a label for the bottles of tequila that he gives as gifts from his studio, Covarrubias was conscious of the importance of the product for the region, and also that tequila is one of the best-known Mexican images internationally. He designed a label that bore not only the word 'tequila' but also 'azul', which, as well as meaning 'blue', is the name of Covarrubias's studio. For a poster entitled *Rehilete* (Windmill) he used a visual trick, based on a detail from a photograph he had taken of the cathedral door in Cologne. He repeated the detail until it formed a windmill, one of his favourite toys as a child. These examples reflect Covarrubias's fondness for using the equivalent of word play in visual form.

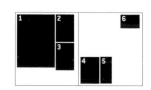

1 *Rehilete* (Windmill), a poster based on details from the door of Cologne Cathedral, 1975
2 *Las Contadoras* (Women accountants), a mixed-media collage for a one-man exhibition in Guadalajara, 2001
3 *Sue'os nocturnos* (Dreams by night), mixed-media collage for a one-man exhibition in Guadalajara, 1999
4 Poster for the Design School at ITESO University in Guadalajara, 2002
5 Illustration for a poster entitled *America 500 Years Later*, 1992
6 Logo for tequila bottles given as gifts from Covarrubias's GaleríAzul studio, 1995

EDGAR REYES RAMÍREZ believes that "developing a contemporary visual culture in Mexico does not mean creating kitsch Mexican curios like the coloured donkeys and zebras that appear in the postcards of Tijuana. Nor does it mean stealing the Aztec and Mayan symbols and using them as company logos, as generations of designers have been doing. Rather, it is about creating an idiosyncratic work for our people using our own codes of communication."

A graduate in Graphic Design from the Benémerita Autonomous University of Puebla in 2000, Reyes Ramírez now works at La Fe Ciega studio in Mexico City with two art directors, Domingo N. Martínez and Yolanda Garibay. The studio's focus is largely on magazine design, and among Reyes Ramírez's current clients are the travel publication *Travesías* and *La Mosca*, which covers rock music. He and his partners have also developed the original designs for the airline magazine *Vuelo de Mexicana*, the electronic-music magazine *URBO1* and the pop-culture publication *Zugo*.

Reyes Ramírez's preferred medium for creating a 'code of communication' is typography, which he has favoured for its expressive potential since his time at university. He likes to use 'modern' typographies, although it has sometimes been difficult to find what he calls "the perfect voice" from what is available, and he has had to create it himself. "Through typography I can personalize my work, make it distinctive," he says. "It is a hobby that allows me to explore different design styles, and in particular vernacular or popular graphics."

During his time at the La Fe Ciega studio, Reyes Ramírez has designed the Synthetic Propaganda typography for *URBO1* magazine, and Euphoria, which is used for the logo of the magazine *Arcana* and also for *Travesías*. Among the more experimental typographies he has created are La Sabrosa, Come Closer, Artificial Beauty Set and Temperamental.

One of Reyes Ramírez's projects outside magazine design has been a postcard series entitled 'Usted no está aquí' (You are not here). This was a collaborative venture involving several young designers from various Mexican cities, the objective being to create a feeling for a place through the personal interpretation of someone who lives there. The themes explored included typical food and products used by the local people, prominent personalities, and objects that have a special significance for each place. "I used a vernacular language," he says, "with graphics similar to those on the walls of the town. The colours are those used regularly by the restaurants, and the typographies are inspired by popular signs, idiomatic expressions, and popular slang, with double meanings in the written messages."

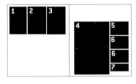

1 La Sabrosa, an experimental typeface, 2000
2 Synthetic Propaganda, a typeface for *URBO1* magazine, 2001
3 Euphoria, a font for the magazines *Arcana* and *Travesias*, 2001
4 Contents page for issue no. 56 of the rock magazine *La Mosca*, 2002
5 Feature page on the group The Cure for *La Mosca* magazine, 2002
6 Postcards from the series 'Usted no está aqui' (You are not here), 2001
7 Cover for the electronic-music magazine *URBO1*, 2001

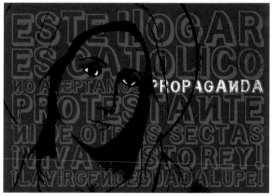

CUADRO DE HORROR EDITOR CURADO JAIME FLORES DIRECTOR INCURABLE HUGO GARCÍA MICHEL REDACCIÓN SMITH MARÍA JOSÉ CORTÉS CONTRERAS ARTE, DISEÑO Y MUCHACHOS QUE NO LLORAN ESTUDIO LA FE CIEGA lafe@adetel.net.mx YOLANDA GARIBAY, DOMINGO NOÉ MARTÍNEZ Y EDGAR REYES COORDINACIÓN GALORE DIANA BARRETO SANTANA PUBLICIDAD DESINTEGRADA LUCÍA AYLUARDO, ROCÍO NAVARRO CORPORATIVO FLOMON ADMINISTRACION ANGÉLICA CASTILLO CIRCULACIÓN VERÓNICA MALDONADO RAMÍREZ PREPRENSA DIGITAL AARÓN OLVERA VILLICAÑA, FERNANDO PEÑA, GABRIEL GARCÍA RANGEL, HUGO RIZO COLABORAN EN ESTE NÚMERO JOSÉ AGUSTÍN, LUIS MIGUEL ARAGÓN, ALEJANDRO ARIZMENDI, NICOLÁS CABRAL, ALEJANDRO CASTRO, MARGARITA CERVIÑO, DAVID CORTÉS, ADRIANA DÍAZ ENCISO, ERICK ESTRADA, GABRIEL FEIJOO, ARTURO J. FLORES, MÓNICA FRÍAS, ROGELIO GARZA, CARLOS JESÚS GONZÁLEZ, FEDRO CARLOS GUILLÉN, ISADORA HASTINGS, ROSA HELLION TOVAR, VÍCTOR MANUEL HIGUERA, MAYRA INZUNZA, ALEJANDRO MAGALLANES, ALBERTO MANGE, KAREM MARTÍNEZ, ALEJANDRO MENDOZA CASASOLA, SERGIO MONSALVO C., JOSÉ XAVIER NÁVAR, PATRICIA PEÑALOZA, CAPITÁN PIJAMA, JOSÉ QUINTERO, XAVIER QUIRARTE, FERNANDO RIVERA CALDERÓN, CONSTANZA ROJAS, GERARDO SIFUENTES, FERNANDA SOLÓRZANO, SUSY Q, SARA VALENZUELA, CLAUDIA VÁZQUEZ, YVONNE VENEGAS, ARMANDO VEGA-GIL, DANNY WAKANTANKA.

LA PASITA BAR
SINGER

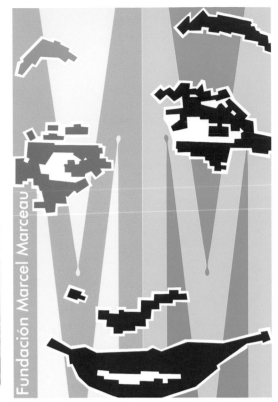

**SANTIAGO POL**

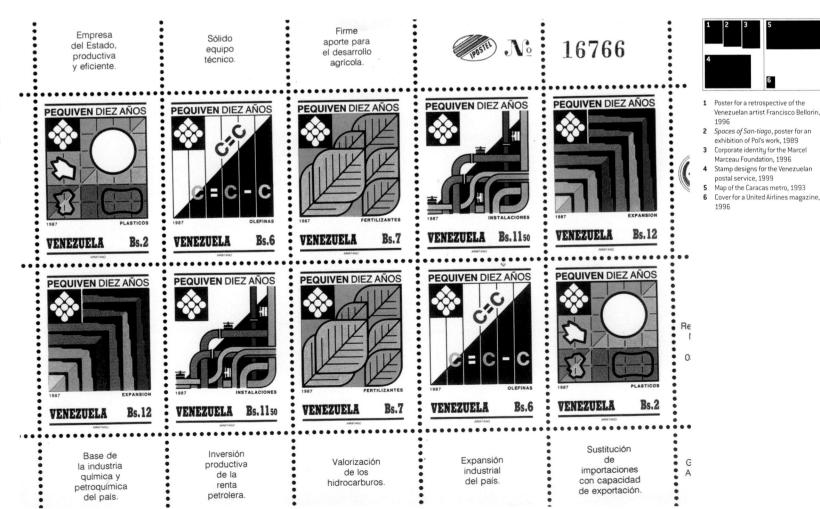

1 Poster for a retrospective of the
Venezuelan artist Francisco Bellorin,
1996
2 *Spaces of San-tiago*, poster for an
exhibition of Pol's work, 1989
3 Corporate identity for the Marcel
Marceau Foundation, 1996
4 Stamp designs for the Venezuelan
postal service, 1999
5 Map of the Caracas metro, 1993
6 Cover for a United Airlines magazine,
1996

PANTEON
Urdaneta
PROPATRIA
Perez Bonalde
Plaza Sucre
Gato Negro
Agua Salud
Caño Amarillo
CAPITOLIO
La Hoyada
Parque Carabobo
Bellas Artes
Colegio de Ingenieros
PLAZA VENEZUELA
Sabana Grande
Chacaíto
Chacao
Altamira
Parque del Este
Los Dos Caminos
Los Cortijos
La California
Petare
PALO VERDE

El Silencio
San Agustin
Capuchinos
Roca Tarpeya
Los Chaguaramos
Maternidad
Los Rosales
Santa Mónica
Artigas
El Valle
LA BANDERA
La Paz
La Yaguara
Los Jardines
Carapita
Coche
Antimano
LA RINCONADA
Mamera
Ruiz Pineda
Caricuao
LAS ADJUNTAS
ZOOLOGICO

LINEA PROPATRIA - PALO VERDE
LINEA CARICUAO - CENTRO
LINEA RINCONADA - PANTEON
LINEA LA BANDERA - PLAZA VENEZUELA

"What is most characteristic of my country is its virgin and exuberant nature, and the fusion of three different races, which contribute their varied interpretations of customs, folklore, colour and symbolism that constantly enrich our visual language." SANTIAGO POL

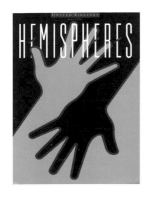

SANTIAGO POL STUDIED fine art at the School of Plastic Arts in Caracas and later at the Ecole Nationale Supérior des Beaux-Arts in Paris. His interest in graphic design developed gradually as a result of jobs he undertook as a student. While studying in Caracas he worked in photolithography in a printing shop, and later he retouched photographs for the Caracas daily newspaper *El Nacional*. During his time as a student in Paris he worked with Victor Vasarely, the French-Hungarian abstract painter. "Because of these varied experiences", he says, "I now apply myself to both graphic art and fine art."

During the 1970s Pol was part of a team of designers that had responsibility for the design of Venezuela's postage stamps. Their modern and dynamic approach led to the creation of what became known as "the new Venezuelan stamp", and the eventual design of more than one hundred examples.

Another landmark graphic-design project for Pol was the creation, in the 1980s, of a representative map for the Caracas Metro. "For this project", he says, "I was able to synthesize beauty, function and simplicity so that it could be used by millions of passengers in the Caracas metro." The map was reproduced until 1998, and the current design follows Pol's original configuration.

Pol's approach to design has been influenced by a number of factors. "My work has been consciously nourished by features of my country Venezuela, its geography, racial mixture, sunlight, and the colours of its flora and fauna. What is most characteristic of my country is its virgin and exuberant nature, and the fusion of three different races, which contribute their varied interpretations of customs, folklore, colour and symbolism that constantly enrich our visual language."

Pol explains that he has been inspired by a number of international masters of the 'plastic arts', including Victor Vasarely, René Magritte and Pablo Picasso, and the North American Pop artists Andy Warhol and Roy Lichtenstein. He points out that he owes a special debt of gratitude to the Venezuelan plastic artists who have guided his development: "Masters of the academic excellence of Gerd Leufert and Nedo are the creators I have most admired, maybe because in Venezuela I was very close to them and shared professional design experiences with them – especially Nedo, with whom I was able to share in the formation of new teaching approaches for design in the School of Plastic Arts of Caracas."

Once Upon a Time, Cinema

a film by: **Mohsen Makhmalbaf**

5

عندما تشعر باقتراب النهاية
and when you feel
you're near the end...
LEBANON 2002

6

reflected in the quality of its graphic designers and their growing international reputations. Bronze Age artefacts in gold, silver and bronze, and ceramics from the ancient Turkish civilizations of Anatolia and Troy, were an important source of this visual tradition. From the fifth to the fifteenth century the Byzantine Empire provided global inspiration for visual artists, writers and musicians, and from the fifth to the eighth century Constantinople (now Istanbul) was considered to be the world's leading centre of art and culture. Islamic influences on Turkish art began in the eighth century and strengthened after the formation of the first Muslim Turkish state in the eleventh century. Throughout most of the twentieth century the political situation in Turkey was unstable, and the country endured a number of international and civil wars. With the exception of a brief period in the late 1960s, industrial development was slow until economic reform policies were introduced in 1983.

The awareness and practice of graphic design in Turkey has also developed slowly, and, as in Iran, this has been partly due to the country's relatively slow rate of industrialization. Also as in Iran, the perceived materialistic values of the West have not been readily embraced by the predominantly Muslim population. While the success of new economic policies has resulted in an increasing output of corporate-identity design, much of the

work of Turkish graphic designers still has a cultural emphasis. Political issues continue to inspire many designers, and this is reflected in the aggressive and fresh political posters of such graphic designers as Memed Erdener, who signs himself 'Extrastruggle'.

Graphic designers from the Middle Eastern countries of Lebanon and Syria have been influenced by their links with European Christian cultures as well as their ties to the Arab world. Approximately 10% of the Syrian population is Christian, while in Lebanon the Christian and Arab numbers are about equal. Syria's visual traditions have been informed by the civilizations of Byzantium and Babylon, and by Islam, and more recently by France, which colonized the country from the early nineteenth century until the Second World War. The influences of each of these cultures have been reflected for centuries in murals, jewellery, mosaics and architecture, but Syria's contemporary visual artists are better known for their work in areas such as caricature and sculpture than for graphic design. Ali Farzat, Geirge Bahjouri, Naji al Ali and Molhem Imad are considered to be among the leading caricaturists of the Middle East, and the black humour of Farzat's caricatures has been an important part of Syrian cultural life since the early 1980s.

Lebanese graphic designer and academic Halim Choueiry discussed some of the challenges facing graphic designers in the Middle East in a 2002

7

editorial for the graphic-design magazine *Comma*. In answer to the question "Does the region have an identifiable visual style?" he replied: "We have come to believe that the West is superior. Therefore, we tend to disregard our own heritage, our visual traditions, our intimate knowledge of our people. We attempt to imitate and incorporate foreign aspects into our work not because they are meaningful to us but because we believe them to be superior to what we have. In doing this, we have become poor imitators."

Choueiry goes on to examine indigenous approaches to visual communication in a number of countries in the Middle East and argues that "the vernacular reveals an intuitive, spontaneous expression driven by immediate need. It is a dialect, a very expressive means of communication by someone without any training but with a direct knowledge of the audience. The vernacular has a freedom which, though unsophisticated and unselfconscious, can be quite direct and powerful … . We can learn from the directness, the freshness, the unpredictable qualities of the vernacular."

The geometrical patterns and colours of the Middle East have had a significant influence on graphic designers around the globe, and many Middle Eastern designers have earned international reputations for their skills in illustration and calligraphy that have been applied mainly in the design of cultural and religious publications.

However, design for manufacturing industry and business corporations has been slow to develop in this region for the reasons outlined above.

The increasing profile of the advertising industry in the Middle East provides encouragement for many graphic designers, but offends others who object to some of the values projected by the industry. The advertising field in Western countries provides numerous opportunities for graphic designers through in-house creative departments and the engagement of freelance graphic designers, and similar opportunities could be provided in the Middle East if the existing resistance to the industry were overcome. The monthly magazine *ArabAd*, which is published in Beirut and covers the advertising industry in Lebanon, Syria, Jordan, Kuwait, Oman, Bahrain, Qatar and the United Arab Emirates, shows that advertising in the Middle East need not reflect a Western visual approach. Vernacular approaches to typography, layout and illustration are apparent in the examples featured in the magazine, which include covers for regional newspapers and magazines, billboard advertisements, packaging, and vehicle branding. A further sign of encouragement for graphic designers in the Middle East was the inclusion in the June 2002 issue of *ArabAd* of a lengthy profile of visual communication and the potential value to the advertising industry of good graphic design.

8

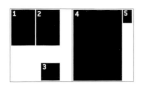

1 Book cover for *The Historical Novels of Iran*, 2002
2 Book cover for the collection of poems *Diwan-e Hafez*, 2002
3 Logo based on five Farsi characters for Doran Publications, 1998
4 Poster for the 7th Biennial of Iranian Graphic Designers, 2002
5 Poster for the book *Graphic Design Iran 1*, 2002

MAJID ABBASI

MAJID ABBASI IS UNSURE WHY he chose graphic design as a career. At high school he was inspired by the work of the Iranian caricaturist Ahmad Sakhavarz, but he was also passionate about music and wanted to be a conductor. He is now glad he took up design, however, and is proud of his achievements. After leaving school, in 1986, he began work as a graphic designer on four Iranian publications, *Cheshmeh*, *Khojasteh*, *Did* and *Fararavan*, despite his parents' concerns about the suitability of graphic design as a career for their son. These publications took a controversial, reformist approach to religious and political themes. In 1991 Abbasi started the graphic-design studio Did Graphics with Firooz Shafei, and also began studying for his BA in Graphic Design at the University of Tehran, graduating in 1996.

In 1996 a co-operative of Iranian designers that included Abbasi founded the Iranian Graphic Designers Society (IGDS), with Morteza Momayez as the first president. Abbasi points out that, although this professional society is fairly new, Iranian graphic designers have been making an impact internationally for about forty years: "Our culture has been influenced by the visual arts for thousands of years, but it is only fairly recently that we have been applying our visual traditions to the design of book covers, posters, magazines and logos. Our designers are determined to use new ways, combining art with Iranian culture and at the same time avoiding clichés."

Abbasi's own design work has been represented in national and international exhibitions and competitions, and has been awarded two national prizes. In 2002 he formed the design group 5th Color with the young Iranian graphic designers Reza Abedini, Saed Meshki, Bijan Sayfuri and Alireza Mostafazedeh. The group's objective is to promote the talents of the new generation of Iranian graphic designers through exhibitions and events that focus on such themes as poster design and typography.

Among Abbasi's most memorable design projects have been his poster for the exhibition entitled *The Keystone: 56 Posters from 8 Iranian Graphic Designers* and his cover design for a collection of poems by the fourteenth-century Iranian poet Hafez. "I gave the poster a strong message by using a yellow background and Farsi and Persian typography," he explains. "For the book cover I used the *nastaligh* style of Persian calligraphy, where marks are added to the Arabic letters to represent sounds that do not occur in Arabic. The background to the book cover is a Persian *termeh*, or decorative textile pattern, found usually in architecture and miniatures."

"Our designers are determined to use new ways, combining art with Iranian culture and at the same time avoiding clichés." MAJID ABBASI

The 7th Biennial of Iranian Graphic Designers

Iranian Graphic Designers (IGDS) with collaboration of Visual Arts Center Presents:
February 12 - March 19, 2002. Niavaran Cultural Center.

REZA ABEDINI

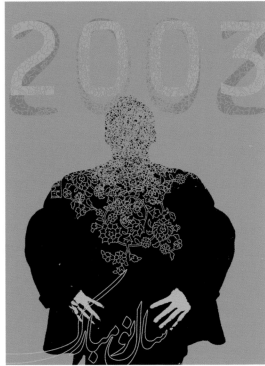

"Traditional calligraphy ... should be the most important element in Iranian design." REZA ABEDINI

REZA ABEDINI, WHO HAS HIS own studio in Tehran, considers himself to be an experimental graphic designer. Before starting his professional design career in 1985, he studied archaeology and monument conservation in Isfahan, Iran, and then painting at the Art University of Tehran. He has earned his reputation as an art director and a graphic designer for his work on numerous magazines, books and film posters, and as a writer, critic and academic in the field of visual arts.

"I have always been fascinated by the visual traditions of my country, particularly by Iranian architecture, miniatures, and the atmosphere of traditional Iranian painting," he says. "There has been a totally distinctive interpretation of art in the Persian culture since ancient times, from the great Achaemenian civilization up to the Islamic era, and this has provided a reference point for my work. I have tried also to focus upon traditional calligraphy, which in my opinion should be the most important element in Iranian design."

Among Abedini's design heroes is fellow country-man Morteza Momayez, whom he describes as "the maestro". Abedini has been particularly influenced by the highly poetic, expressive and resonant quality of Momayez's work, and by his visual power and intelligence. According to Abedini, although historically graphic design in Iran has been illustrative, in recent years a number of young Iranian designers have emerged to focus more on design content and to create a design language of their own.

Two of Abedini's design projects provide an insight into his approach. One is his poster commemorating the great thirteenth-century Iranian poet and intellectual Mowlavi, for an exhibition in 2001 at Marc Bloch University in Strasbourg. "Whenever I work on a project like this", he says, "I become very excited by the poster, and completely absorbed in it. I knew that my audience would be a varied one, including French visitors to the exhibition, Iranians living abroad, and Mowlavi experts. As in all my work, I was trying to look at the subject from a fresh angle. I was sensitive to the traditional forms of religious dance that are part of the Mowlavi mysticism, and I wanted to convey a feeling for this. I tried also to focus on traditional Persian typography that is derived from classical Iranian calligraphy."

The other project is a cover for the book *A Tale of Dwarfs and Lankier*. The text is a political satire, and as the book is full of images Abedini decided to invert the normal Iranian approach to cover design, where the emphasis is on illustration or photography, by using typography almost exclusively. He manipulated the common fonts and accompanied them with simple images, and he described as "strange and unorthodox" his use of scale and spacing for the names of the author and designer.

1   Poster for an international colloquium and exhibition commemorating the thirteenth-century Iranian poet Mowlavi, 2001
2   Book cover for *Resaleh Delgosha*, a selection of ancient satirical poems, 1999
3   Greetings card, 2003
4   Editorial spread for *Tasvir*, a graphic-design magazine, 1998
5   Cover for the magazine of the Iranian Cultural Heritage Organization, 1997
6   Book cover for *A Tale of Dwarfs and Lankier*, 1999

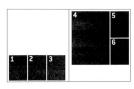

1   Poster to promote the play
    *Savoushoun*, 2000
2   Cover of a brochure promoting the film
    *The Cyclist*, directed by Mohsen
    Makhmalbaf, 1990
3   Book jacket for a volume of poems,
    1999
4   Poster to commemorate the
    hundredth anniversary of the birth of
    the Iranian poet Nima Yushij, 1996
5   Cover of a brochure promoting the film
    *O! Iran*, directed by Naser Taghvai,
    1990
6   Cover for the magazine *Journey*, 2000

THE RENOWNED IRANIAN graphic designer Ebrahim Haghighi has won numerous international awards for his work in poster design, illustration, painting, engraving and lithography, as well as film direction and design. He is Professor of Graphic Arts at the University of Tehran, a member of the board of the Iranian Graphic Designers Society (IGDS) and a member of the AGI (Alliance Graphique Internationale).

Professor Haghighi explains his lifelong interest in the interaction of the many forms of visual art in an article for the October 2000 issue of *Jahat-e-Etelae* (the IGDS newsletter): "Photography, cinema and graphic design", he says, "are the same-aged children of the Image Family. These three young children, whose mother is painting, have stepped into the twenty-first century wearing each others' clothes. Photographs appear with a graphic look, graphic designs appear in the form of cinema which is made up of moving photographs. During their short lives they have undergone changes in their forms and conditions many times, and they are going to transform in a bizarre way in the information and digital world."

Haghighi's love of painting led to his studying architecture at the University of Tehran, and it was here that he developed "a serious interest in graphic design". He explains that Iran has a history of visual art that has spanned more than 5000 years, and he is grateful for his college education, which exposed him to miniature painting, tilework, ornamental design and its application to architecture, Persian carpets and calligraphy – "such national wealth". "There is such a vast field", he says, "that a designer or artist can grasp only part of it." He names as his main influences two Iranian masters, Morteza Momayez and Farshid Mesghali; the former he regards as the founder of modern Iranian graphic design.

Since the early 1990s Haghighi has been using Persian calligraphy in his work. He feels that graphic design that uses the ancient script skilfully has great potential for influencing human behaviour. This is due to the traditional Islamic belief in the spiritual relationship between calligraphy, the Koran and the true nature of God. Among his favourite projects is his design, in 1995, of a poster to commemorate the hundredth anniversary of the birth of Nima Yushij, the founder of modern Persian poetry. "While he influenced our contemporary poetry quite dramatically", says Haghighi, "he had to fight against the strong establishment of old poetry. In my design for the poster his image is hidden in the darkness of night, but in contrast I have employed colourful fireworks to express visually how his poetry functioned during his time and since his death. The work of Nima Yushij lightens everyone's mind, and in catching your glance lends you new sight."

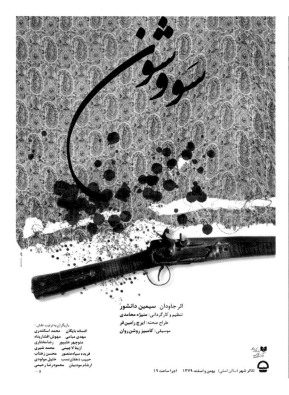

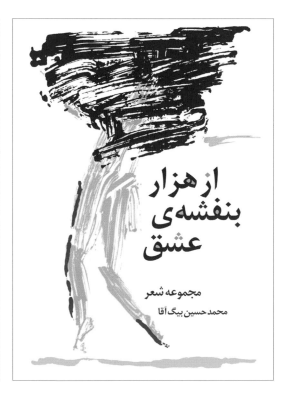

"Photography, cinema and graphic design are the same-aged children of the Image Family. These three young children, whose mother is painting, have stepped into the twenty-first century wearing each others' clothes." EBRAHIM HAGHIGHI

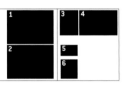

**1** Poster for a survey of contemporary Iranian cinema, 2003
**2** Poster for the 4th International Theatre Festival of Iranzamin, 2002
**3** Poster for a concert by the ensemble Constantinople, 2002
**4** Cover for *Lost Paradises*, a book of poems by Jorge Luis Borges, 2002
**5** Title design for the magazine *Aftab* (Sunlight), 2000
**6** Logo for the ensemble Constantinople, 2002

> "The focus on poetry has caused the art of calligraphy to flourish: we have masterpieces in calligraphy that are very similar to paintings."
> SAED MESHKI

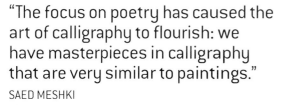

"BEFORE ANYTHING ELSE IT was the climate and culture of ancient Persia that impressed me," says Saed Meshki, Iranian graphic designer and member of the Alliance Graphique Internationale (AGI) and the Iranian Graphic Designers Society (IGDS). "I was born beside the desert in a land where the sun shines so brightly that even colourful objects have no contrast with the natural environment. It's so calm and silent, and because of its clearness the night sky is seen close to the earth."

Having studied theatre, calligraphy, music, graphic design, painting and drawing at the Teacher Training College in Tehran, Meshki entered the Faculty of Arts at the University of Tehran in the late 1980s. He began working professionally as a designer from that time, drawing much of his inspiration from the animated films, film posters and children's book illustration of the Iranian master Farshid Mesghali.

Meshki has a particular interest in the history of the visual culture of his country, and has studied the development of graphic design since the 1960s. Following a "fabulous period" between 1966 and 1979, there was a gap of some years as a result of the revolution in Iran. According to Meshki, in the last few years a new generation of graphic designers has presented a modern view of Iranian design that is still developing. These designers are more willing than their predecessors to explore secular themes and to show the influences of modern art in their work.

Literature, claims Meshki, dominates all the arts in Iran, and nowhere else in the world is poetry so intertwined with the lives of the people. "Because the visual arts have always been under the influence of literature," he says, "illustration has been more popular than painting. The focus on poetry has caused the art of calligraphy to flourish: we have masterpieces in calligraphy that are very similar to paintings." Ancient Persian calligraphy, along with Persian myths and Iranian classical music, has inspired Meshki's work. "I'm also very interested in the culture of my fathers, in Zoroaster and his religious beliefs," he says.

In 1992 Meshki designed the logo and other promotional material for the music ensemble Constantinople. The group plays music from the Middle Ages and Renaissance using early European and Middle Eastern instruments – some of them Persian – and has made a careful study of the classical Persian tradition. "For the logo, I designed a bird in a frame that seemed like a musical instrument – a harp," he explains. "For the logotype, I altered an ancient Persian text. I spent a lot of time thinking of how to combine European paintings and engravings from the Middle Ages with those of the same era from Iran. I wanted the work to seem ancient and modern at the same time. I think I succeeded."

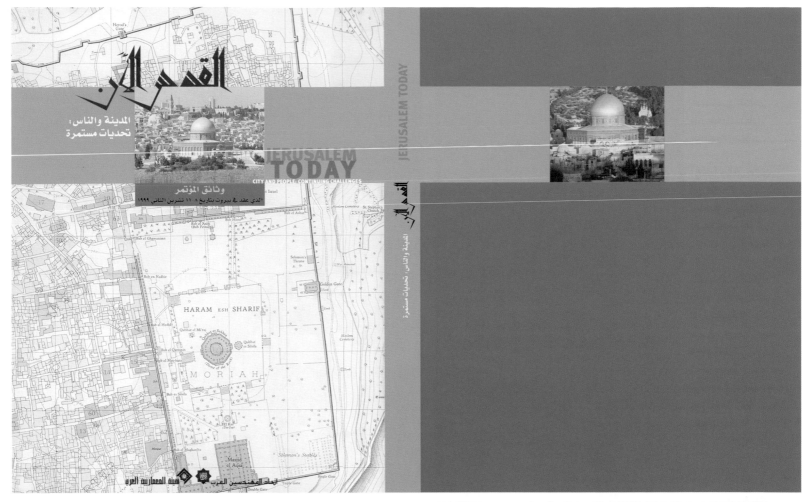

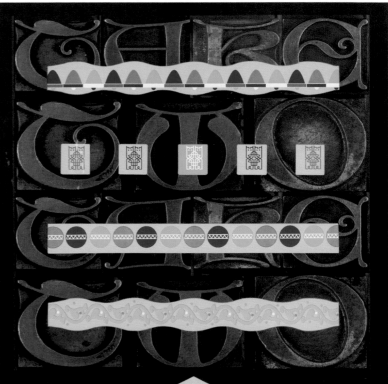

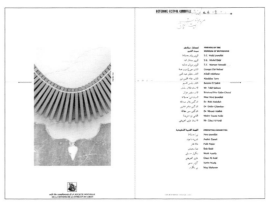

> "I have always felt that Post-modernism fits the Lebanese culture, since it is multifaceted, layered, and full of contrasts and contradictions." LEILA MUSFY

PROFESSOR LEILA MUSFY IS the Director of the Graphic Design Program at the American University of Beirut, and a partner at Taketwo [Designhaus] in Beirut. She studied design in the United States, earning her BFA in 1978 from Kansas City Art Institute and her MFA in 1981 from Cranbrook Academy of Art, Michigan. She regards as her mentor the architect and industrial designer Victor Papanek, author of the 1972 book *Design for the Real World: Human Ecology and Social Change*, which advocates socially responsible design.

Professor Musfy feels that her particular approach, which explores the notions of universal language and universality in design, stems from the fact that she has links with both Lebanese and American cultures. "Language is an important issue to address," she says. "For instance, most Lebanese people use at least two languages from Arabic, French and English. The languages have different aesthetic rules, different directions and sometimes different meanings. Solutions cannot come out of a formula or a logical equation. Solutions normally stem from creativity. My approach is to take the spirit of the past and combine it with a full understanding of the present by means of creativity. As I am an educator, designer and painter, I find it difficult to dissociate one field from another."

In addition, Professor Musfy explains: "I have always felt that Post-modernism fits the Lebanese culture, since it is multifaceted, layered, and full of contrasts and contradictions. It is traditional on the one hand and modern on the other."

Between 1994 and 1997, the design of catalogues for the Beiteddine Festival in Lebanon formed a significant project for Musfy. Beiteddine, the eighteenth-century palace of Arab princes and a historical site, stages a wide range of performances each year. When designing the catalogue in the first year, Musfy's primary objective was to establish an image for the festival. "I followed my constant design approach, which is to establish a theme and then pursue active research and experimentation," she explains. "The nature of the project allowed for freedom, as the festival activity is art itself. The project allowed me to experiment in the way of a fine artist. The catalogue page became a canvas, and I was able to open up a lot of possibilities by playing with colours, weights and forms. My love of typography gave another layer to my work, and I was able to test possibilities by juxtaposing Arabic and Latin scripts. This has allowed me to address the issues that concern me most, namely universal language versus identity, heritage versus technology, and adaptation versus craft."

1 Screen-saver promoting tourism in
   Syria, 2000
2 Cover for a CD promoting the Dubai
   International Award for Best Practices
   to Improve the Living Environment,
   2001
3 Promotional graphic for arabesK
   digital arts, 1996
4 Website for the five-star Zenobia
   Desert Camp near the Palmyra ruins
   in Syria, 2000
5 Website for Atlas Tours, 1999
6 Title page of a monthly digital guide
   for the American Cultural Center in
   Damascus, 2003

LAMINE BENSAOU

WHILE STUDYING MEDICINE IN Syria in 1980, Lamine Bensaou decided to take up graphic design. "From a young age I had been impressed by the advertisements in foreign magazines and newspapers that arrived in my country," he says. "I felt that the challenge was there for us to create similar visual imagery for our own culture and our own market." He embraced the challenge and took courses in graphic design at a private institute, quickly becoming interested in digital imagery. Once he had gained some professional experience he founded his own studio, arabesK digital arts, a conceptual digital graphic-solutions firm in the Syrian capital, Damascus.

Bensaou has played a significant part in raising awareness of graphic design in Syria. He was Head of the Department of Graphic Design at the Reda Computer Centre in Damascus for ten years, and continues to teach digital imaging and graphic design. He is conscious that Syria has been the 'cradle' for several great civilizations, and that it has rich visual traditions. "All these civilizations have left us rich treasures of visual experience that have more significance for graphic art and design than academic theoretical knowledge," he says. "I consider that the most important part of my experience has been acquired from the hybrid of new digital technologies and the vestiges of art from our past great civilizations."

The most distinctive element of Syrian graphic design, Bensaou believes, is the variety of colour. He explains that this emanates from the incredible environment of natural colours found in any corner of Syria. "Because of the distinctive features of our landscape and our heritage", he adds, "we have a great opportunity to combine traditional photography with digital technology, to offer competitive and creative imaging not always possible with traditional photography alone."

Bensaou's studio focuses on design for the tourist industry, for which it creates logos, catalogues, packaging, and magazine and newspaper advertisements. The firm publishes a weekly electronic newsletter that features articles on Syrian culture, history and travel. Its Syria Seek website provides news about travel, and Caravan 2 Syria offers a chat room for travellers.

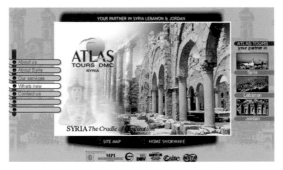

"The most important part of my experience has been acquired from the hybrid of new digital technologies and the vestiges of art from our past great civilizations."
LAMINE BENSAOU

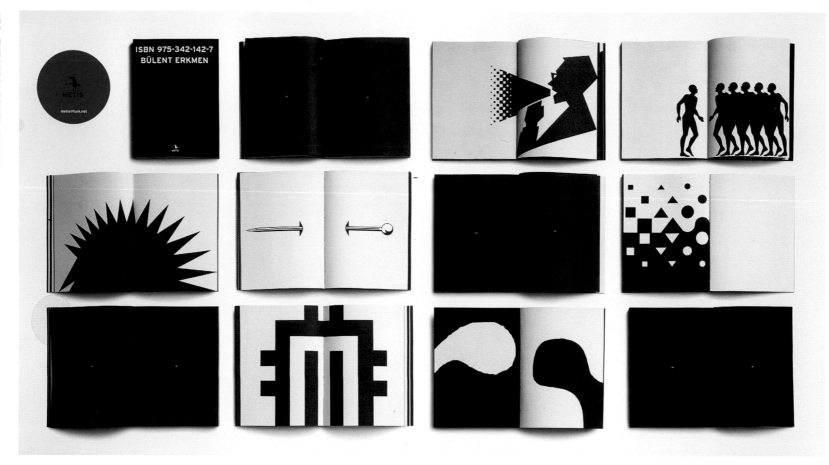

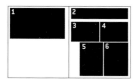

1  Poster for a series of books by the Modernist writer Sevim Burak, 1994
2  Logo for a series of books by Sevim Burak, 1994
3  Aids poster for the Lambda group, 1994
4  Poster for the cultural and political project 'Sharing Jerusalem: Two Capitals for Two States', 1998
5  Poster designed in response to a challenge from Israeli designer David Tartakover, 2000
6  Cover for the architecture and design magazine *Arredamento*, 2000

BULENT ERKMEN HAS BEEN practising graphic design since his graduation from the Istanbul State Academy of Fine Arts in 1972. His work has been published in *Graphis* magazine, and more than eighty of his works are in the permanent design collections of museums in France, Germany, Finland, Poland, Switzerland and the United States. He has held exhibitions of his work both at home and abroad, and has won numerous design awards.

According to Erkmen: "Visual imagery in Turkey is a complicated mixture, with many varieties. It can be very colourful and very uncolourful at the same time, with images sometimes overlapping each other and sometimes following each other in linear fashion ...

"My own approach to graphic design is to treat it as a spatial construction, as a structure to be built. It is time to oppose the pretty/not pretty polarity. A good form comes with a good idea, and to resort to ornamentation and decoration when a good idea cannot be found is just a form of escape. Style cannot be chosen; style can only evolve. One should stay away from a descriptive and explanatory graphic design and produce new ways of comprehending and perceiving, rather than new forms or new images. Besides, smell can be music, as can a creaking door. Standing still can be dancing, eating does not mean filling oneself, and making love does not mean reaching an orgasm."

Erkmen's idea of using pins as the theme in a logo design for a series of books came from the working practice of the author, the Modernist writer Sevim Burak. Erkmen explains that Burak writes in fragments, and attaches each paper fragment to the curtains of her room with pins, afterwards changing the arrangements to create new montages. The pins play an important part in the writing process, and she asks friends travelling abroad to bring back pins as gifts.

The idea for a poster entitled *I'm here, where my stones are ...* came from a challenge by the Israeli graphic designer David Tartakover, who sent Erkmen and other designers an image of a Palestinian child throwing stones at an Israeli tank. Tartakover had placed the words "I am here" in the middle of the image, and his challenge to other designers was "Where are you?". "In my poster", says Erkmen, "I wanted to say that my works are my arms, my stones. This is all I have, and with these stones in my pocket may I be in every place where I am expected to be (or not expected to be) and where I am supposed to be."

"It is time to oppose the pretty/not pretty polarity." BÜLENT ERKMEN

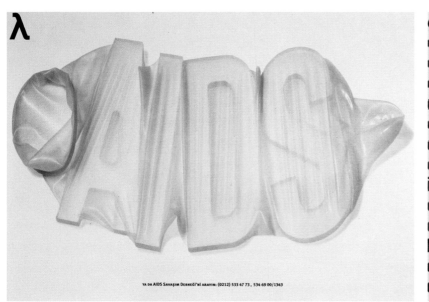

λ

YA DA AIDS Savaşım Derneği'ni arayın: (0212) 533 47 73 , 534 69 00/1343

e.qual (ēʹkwəl) adj [Lat. aequalis ‹ aequus even.] 1. Having the same measure, quantity, or value as another. 2. Math. Being the same or identical to in value. 3 a. Having the same rights, privileges, or status; equality of flaws. b. Being the same for all members of a group of society; employees without chance. 4 a. Having the qualities, as strength, intelligence, or ability, needed for a situation or task. b. Sufficient in extent, amount, or degree. — n. One equal to another. — v. equaled, equaling, equals or equalled, equalling, equals. 1. To be equal to, esp. in value. 2. To do or produce something equal to...

I'm here, where my stones are...

FROM: BÜLENT ERKMEN/İSTANBUL TO: DAVID TARTAKOVER/TEL AVIV

ARREDAMENTO
MİMARLIK

TASARIM KÜLTÜRÜ DERGİSİ
1999/10   900 000 TL

PROFİL:
ÇAĞDAŞ
YUNAN
MİMARLIĞI

DOSYA:
MARMARA DEPREMI

90'LI YILLARDA
SANAT

BALTIMORE
SIRAKONUTLARI

AÇI İLKÖĞRETİM
OKULU

"UN-PRIVATE HOUSE"

PEYZAJ TASARIMCISI
9+1

CARTIER-BRESSON

FASILLAR ANITI

VENEDİK BİENALİ

COMPEX FUARI
DAVETİYESİ

ISSN 1300-3801   10

9 871300 380000

**EXTRASTRUGGLE (MEMED ERDENER)**

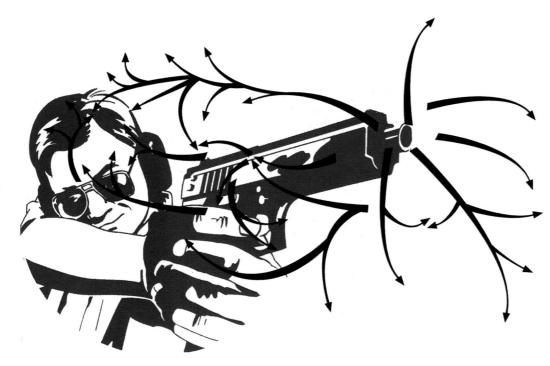

1 *Unexpected Accident*, one of a series of political posters, 1997
2 *Whomsoever the Heart Loves*, a poster on a political theme, 2000
3 *Dream without Vowels*, a poster on a political theme, 2001
4 *Trakonia*, a poster on a political theme, 2001
5 *Afraid of God*, a poster on a religious/political theme, 2001
6 *Fight for Bread*, an illustration for a political campaign, 2001

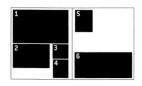

UTA NI

YO RUM

"I'm afraid. Afraid of God." | Turkey 2001 | **EXTRASTRUGGLE**

"To live in Turkey is like living between two open windows that represent text and image."
EXTRASTRUGGLE (MEMED ERDENER)

MEMED ERDENER INSISTS that the word 'Extrastruggle' ('Extramucadele' in Turkish) appears before his name each time his work is acknowledged. The word reflects the focus of his work and his consuming passion, the political situation in Turkey. Erdener is forging a reputation as a member of an exciting new brigade of Turkish graphic designers of Islamic origin.

It is often said that Islamic art and design are characterized by a unification of style and purpose, and that an overall coherence can be identified regardless of region. Calligraphy has been recognized as the most significant element of Islamic visual expression as a result of its traditional association with the Koran. It is interesting to look at the work of young designers such as Erdener in the context of this tradition.

In his political posters Erdener works in only two colours, red and black. These colours represent for him the colours of Extrastruggle. As he puts it: "The behaviour of Turkish politicians convinced me that I had to do something, even if only one thing." A recent edition of the Turkish magazine *Yurtan Sesler* featured three pages of his political statements in the familiar red and black, but they were characterized by a fresh and innovative approach to the blending of calligraphy and pictogram.

"To live in Turkey", says Erdener, "is like living between two open windows that represent text and image. The traditional fonts of the Arabic alphabet are open to continuous variation, and provide a great opportunity to combine calligraphy and pictogram to form what I call the 'caligram'. To write the word 'tiger' so that it looks like a tiger and retains its religious significance is what this is all about, and is the true meaning of this thing called graphic design."

Another side to Erdener's work was seen at the *All Day/Everyday* exhibition held in Istanbul in 2001. The purpose of the exhibition, in the words of the catalogue, was "to show a selection of work from a relatively young generation of artists from Istanbul". Erdener demonstrated his skill in the innovative use of images and technologies, framing a series of computer-manipulated images in glossy plastic embroidery. He showed again that he clearly enjoys playing with traditional forms, superimposing photographic images on to illustrations and adding further graphic elements in the form of clichéd sentences and aphorisms. As the exhibition catalogue states, the images "blast off"!

BURCU KAYALAR, CURRENTLY the Chair of the Board of Directors of the Turkish Society of Graphic Designers (GMK), graduated with a Bachelor of Industrial Design degree from the Middle East Technical University (METU) in Ankara in 1992, and then completed a BA in Graphic Design at the University of California, Los Angeles (UCLA). After graduating from UCLA in 1994 she worked for brief periods in several graphic-design studios in California before returning to Turkey to practise as a freelance graphic designer.

"Most of my fellow graduates in industrial design from METU went on to study either interior design or graphic design, because there were not many job opportunities for industrial designers in Turkey," says Kayalar. "This was due to the low level of manufacturing industry in the country. I saw an opportunity for freelance practice in graphic design, as most of the graphic designers in Turkey worked for advertising agencies, and still do."

Kayalar first set up practice in the capital city, Ankara, where most of her work was on publication design for the government departments based there. After a year she decided to relocate to Istanbul, where most of Turkey's industry and large corporations were located, and where she felt there would be more opportunities for graphic designers. She says: "While an increasing amount of my work in Istanbul has been in the area of corporate design, particularly identity design and promotional material, most of my clients are from the cultural sector, and include publishers and musicians.

"I have a record-label client, Kalan Muzik, which focuses on ethnic music in Turkey and is highly respected. I had already designed two CD covers for the company, and when it formed an association with a record company in The Netherlands it contacted me and asked me to design a suitable logo. So I conceived the idea of 'connecting cultures' to reflect the ethnic nature of the company and its music, with the interlocking colours in the logo symbolizing the different cultures that have been brought together."

When designing a series of wine labels, catalogues and wine lists for Melen Winery of Thrace, in northwest Turkey, Kayalar tried to respond to the request to give them a 'sporty' look: "The client asked me what I thought about the use of blue bottles, and although my first reaction was that they looked like vodka bottles rather than wine bottles, I was able to produce appropriate graphics, which got a very good response from the market. Also, it gave me the opportunity to work with a brush and ink, which is rare nowadays."

"While an increasing amount of my work in Istanbul has been in the area of corporate design ... most of my clients are from the cultural sector, and include publishers and musicians." BURCU KAYALAR

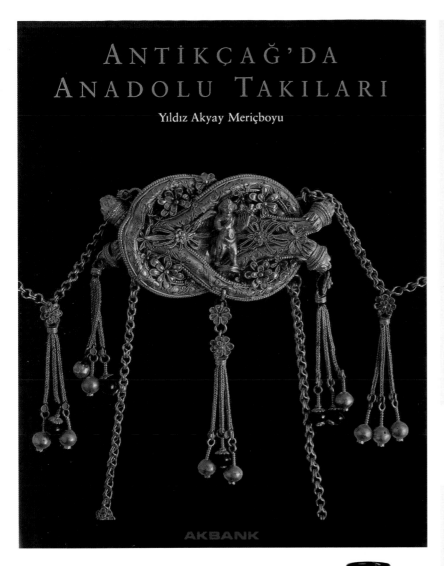

ANTİKÇAĞ'DA
ANADOLU TAKILARI

Yıldız Akyay Meriçboyu

AKBANK

DOĞU ÖĞRETİLERİ

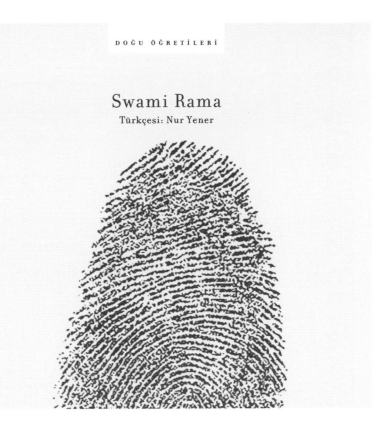

Swami Rama
Türkçesi: Nur Yener

< karma Bağından özgürleşmek >

OKYANUS

CONNECTING CULTURES

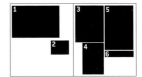

1   Catalogue and restaurant wine list for
    Melen Winery of Thrace, northwest
    Turkey, 2003
2   CD cover for the record company Kalan
    Muzik and the band Kardes Turkuler,
    2002
3   Jacket for a book on antique jewellery
    from Anatolia, 2000
4   Wine label for Melen Winery, 2003
5   Jacket for a book by Swami Rama on
    Eastern philosophy, 2001
6   Logo for a Turkish–Dutch record
    company, 2003

**156 FURTHER READING**

John Barnicoat, *Posters: A Concise History*, London (Thames & Hudson) 1998

Miles Danby, *Moorish Style*, London (Phaidon Press) 1995

Barry Dawson, *Street Graphics India*, London (Thames & Hudson) 1999

M. Dietz and M. Monninger, *Japan Design*, Germany (Benedikt Taschen Verlag) 1992

Ticio Escobar, 'Issues in Popular Art', in G. Mosquera (ed.), *Beyond the Fantastic: Contemporary Art Criticism from Latin America*, London (Institute of Visual Arts) 1992

J. Fraser, S. Heller and S. Chwast, *Japanese Modern: Graphic Design between the Wars*, San Francisco (Chronicle Books) 1996

Jennifer Harris, *5000 Years of Textiles*, London (British Museum Press) 1993

Steven Heller, *Graphic Style: From Victorian to Post-modern*, New York (Harry N. Abrams) 1998

Steven Heller, 'Intervention: Design and Politics/Politics and Design', address to the AIGA National Design Conference, 23 March 2002

Victor Margolin, *The Struggle for Utopia*, Chicago (University of Chicago Press) 1997

Philip Meggs, *A History of Graphic Design*, New York (Van Nostrand Reinhold) 1992

Gerardo Mosquera (ed.), *Beyond the Fantastic: Contemporary Art Criticism from Latin America*, London (Institute of Visual Arts) 1995

R. Pakbaz and Y. Emdadian, *Pioneers of Iranian Modern Art*, Tehran (Tehran Museum of Contemporary Art) 2001

Edward J. Sullivan, *Brazil Body and Soul*, New York (The Solomon R. Guggenheim Foundation) 2001

Richard Thornton, *Japanese Graphic Design*, London (Laurence King Publishing) 1991

Kasra Vadafari, *Iranian Zoroastrians*, Iran (Mahriz Publications) 2002

D. Whitten and N. Whitten, *From Myth to Creation: Art from Amazonian Ecuador*, Chicago (University of Illinois Press) 1988

Frank Willett, *African Art: An Introduction*, New York (Thames & Hudson) 1993

Sue Williamson, *Resistance Art in South Africa*, South Africa (David Philip Publishing) 1989

## AFRICA

**AJMEET BHARIJ, KENYA**
ajmeet@tbwacreative.com

**'SEGUN OLUDE, NIGERIA**
solude@total.net

**ROY CLUCAS, SOUTH AFRICA**
roy@designprocess.co.za

**MICHAEL STALLENBERG, SOUTH AFRICA**
michael@interactive.africa.com

**GARTH WALKER, SOUTH AFRICA**
garth@oj.co.za

**MICHAEL DANES, ZIMBABWE**
design@ecoweb.co.zw

**SAKI MAFUNDIKWA, ZIMBABWE**
sakimaf@hotmail.com

**CHAZ MAVIYANE-DAVIES, ZIMBABWE**
maviyane@comcast.net

## THE FAR EAST

**FANG CHEN, CHINA**
fchen@stu.edu.cn

**WANG XU, CHINA**
sasa@wangxu.com.cn

**SHANKAR BARUA, INDIA**
shankarbaba@vsnl.net

**ITU CHAUDHURI, INDIA**
icdesign@vsnl.com

**TANIA DAS GUPTA, INDIA**
taniajee@hotmail.com

**SUDARSHAN DHEER, INDIA**
dheergrd@vsnl.com

**TAKASHI AKIYAMA, JAPAN**
akiyama@t3.rim.or.jp

**KEIZO MATSUI, JAPAN**
Keizo@100design.com

**U.G. SATO, JAPAN**
ugsato@kt.rim.or.jp

**TADANORI YOKOO, JAPAN**
yokoo@s2.ocv.ne.jp

**KUM NAM BAIK, KOREA**
kumnam@skku.ac.kr

**JAE SIK KWON, KOREA**
iconstudio@hanmail.net

**PRASEUTH BANCHONGPHAKDY, LAOS**
praseuth@laopdr.com

**JOSEPH FOO, MALAYSIA**
joseph.foo@3nitydesign.com

**JACKSON TAN, SINGAPORE**
info@phunkstudio.com

**SU TSUNG-HSIUNG (Jeffrey Su), Taiwan**
lemony@ms24.hinet.net

**PUNLARP PUNNOTOK, Thailand**
punlarp@hotmail.com

**PIUS EUGENE, Vietnam**
kcpius@hcm.fpt.vn

## LATIN AMERICA

**RICARDO DRAB, Argentina**
estudio06@rdya.com.ar

**PABLO KUNST, Argentina**
kunstdcv@satlink.com

**VERONICA D'OREY, Brazil**
vdo@veronicadorey.com.br

**ALESSANDRA MIGANI, Brazil**
alessandramigani@alessa.com.br

**FELIPE TABORDA, Brazil**
felipe.taborda@pobox.com

**ANDRÉS CORREA ILLANES, Chile**
acorreaill@yahoo.com

**CRISTIAN ORDÓÑEZ, Chile**
cristian@h23.cl

**DAVID CONSUEGRA, Colombia**
davidconsuegra@yahoo.com

**JOSÉ 'PEPE' MENÉNDEZ, Cuba**
pepemendez@hotmail.com

**SANTIAGO PUJOL, Cuba**
spujol@cubarte.cult.cu

**ÑIKO (Antonio Pérez Gonzáles), Cuba/Mexico**
amarillo@gorsa.net.mx

**JUAN LORENZO BARRAGÁN, Ecuador**
jlorenzo@hoy.ne

**SILVIO & SANDRO GIORGI, Ecuador**
giotto@treones.com

**ANTONIO MENA, Ecuador**
menamora@ecuanex.net.ec

**XAVIER BERMÚDEZ, Mexico**
tramavis@prodigy.net.mx

**FELIPE COVARRUBIAS, Mexico**
felipec@megared.net.mx

**EDGAR REYES RAMÍREZ, Mexico**
fabrikavisual@yahoo.com

**SANTIAGO POL, Venezuela**
santiagopol@tutopia.com

## THE MIDDLE EAST

**MAJID ABBASI, Iran**
art-director@didgraphics.com

**REZA ABEDINI, Iran**
info@rezaabedini.com

**EBRAHIM HAGHIGHI, Iran**
e.haghighi@kavosh.net

**SAED MESHKI, Iran**
saed@sinasoft.net

**HALIM CHOUEIRY, Lebanon**
hchoueiry@lau.edu.lb

**LEILA MUSFY, Lebanon**
lmusfy@cyberia.net.lb

**LAMINE BENSAOU, Syria**
manager@arabesk-img.com

**BULENT ERKMEN, Turkey**
bulenterkmen@bek.com.tr

**EXTRASTRUGGLE (Memed Erdener), Turkey**
memed_erdener@tr.yr.com

**BURCU KAYALAR, Turkey**
burcukayalar@turk.net

**PAGE 7**
Design and photography: Edgar Reyes

**PAGE 8**
**1** Design: Majid Abbasi
**2** Design: Saki Mafundikwa; Photography:
Dirk Vardenberk

**PAGE 9**
**3** Design: Fang Chen
**4** Design: U.G. Sato
**5** Design: Keizo Matsui

**PAGE 10**
**6** Design: Ricardo Drab

**PAGE 11**
**7** Illustration: David Consuegra
**8** Design: Garth Walker; Copy: Alex Sudheim

**PAGE 12**
**9** Design: Itu Chaudhuri
**10** Design: Jeffrey Su
**11** Design: Jackson Tan, Alvin Tan, William Chan,
Melvin Chee; Photography: Simon

**PAGE 13**
**12** Design: Halim Choueiry
**13** Design: Extrastruggle M. Erdener

**PAGE 14**
**14** Design: Ajmeet Bharij
**15** Design: Antonio Mena

**PAGE 15**
**16** Design: Reza Abedini
**17** Design: Veronica d'Orey

**PAGE 17**
Design: C. Maviyane-Davies

**PAGE 18**
Design and illustration: Ajmeet Bharij

**PAGE 20**
**1** Design: C. Maviyane-Davies
**2** Design: Roy Clucas, Sean Harrison

**PAGE 21**
**3** Design: Michael Stallenberg

**PAGE 22**
**4** Design and illustration: Ajmeet Bharij

**PAGE 23**
**5** Design: Saki Mafundikwa; Art Direction: Charles
Rue Woods

**PAGES 24–25**
**1–3, 5** Design and illustration: Ajmeet Bharij
**4, 6** Design: Ajmeet Bharij

**PAGES 26–27**
**1– 5** Design: 'Segun Olude

**PAGES 28–29**
**1, 3–5** Design: Roy Clucas
**2** Design: Roy Clucas, David Holland, Dan Mathews

**PAGES 30–31**
**1–5** Design: Michael Stallenberg

**PAGES 32–33**
**1–3, 6, 7** Design: Garth Walker
**4** Design: Garth Walker; Copy: Steve Kotze
**5** Design: Garth Walker; Siobhan Gunning

**PAGES 34–35**
**1–3, 6** Design: Michael Danes
**5** Design and photography: Michael Danes

**PAGES 36–37**
**1** Design: Saki Mafundikwa; Photography:
Dirk Vardenberk
**2, 4, 5** Design: Saki Mafundikwa
**3** Design: Saki Mafundikwa; Photography:
Mercedes Sayagues, Calvin Dundo

**PAGES 38–39**
**1** Design: C. Maviyane-Davies
**2, 7** Design: C. Maviyane-Davies; Photography:
Ian Murphy, Rolf Varga
**3, 6** Design: C. Maviyane-Davies; Photography:
Ian Murphy
**4** Design: C. Maviyane-Davies; Photography:
Alex Joe
**5** Design: C. Maviyane-Davies

**PAGE 41**
Printmaker: Kum Nam Baik

**PAGE 42**
Design: Fang Chen

**PAGE 44**
**1** Design: Fang Chen
**2** Design: Wang Xu
**3** Design: Studio of Pius Eugene

**PAGE 45**
**4** Design: Tania Das Gupta
**5** Design: Takashi Akiyama

**PAGE 46**
**6** Design: Keizo Matsui
**7** Design: Tadanori Yokoo

**PAGE 47**
**8** Design: Kum Nam Baik
**9** Design: Jae Sik Kwon
**10** Design: Joseph Foo, Kam Wei, Wei Ming;
Photography: Patrick

**PAGES 48–49**
**1–5** Design: Fang Chen

**PAGES 50–51**
**1–5** Design: Wang Xu

**PAGES 52–53**
**1** Design and photography: Shankar Barua
**2, 3** Design: Shankar Barua

**PAGES 54–55**
**1–6** Design: Itu Chaudhuri

**PAGES 56–57**
**1–3** Design: Tania Das Gupta

**PAGES 58–59**
**1–5** Design: Sudarshan Dheer

**PAGES 60–61**
**1–6** Design: Takashi Akiyama

**PAGES 62–63**
**1–6** Design: Keizo Matsui

**PAGES 64–65**
**1–7** Design: U.G. Sato

**PAGES 66–67**
**1–5** Design: Tadanori Yokoo

**PAGES 68–69**
**1–4** Design: Kum Nam Baik

**PAGES 70–71**
**1–6** Design: Jae Sik Kwon